I0804990

POSTCARD HISTORY SERIES

Oshkosh

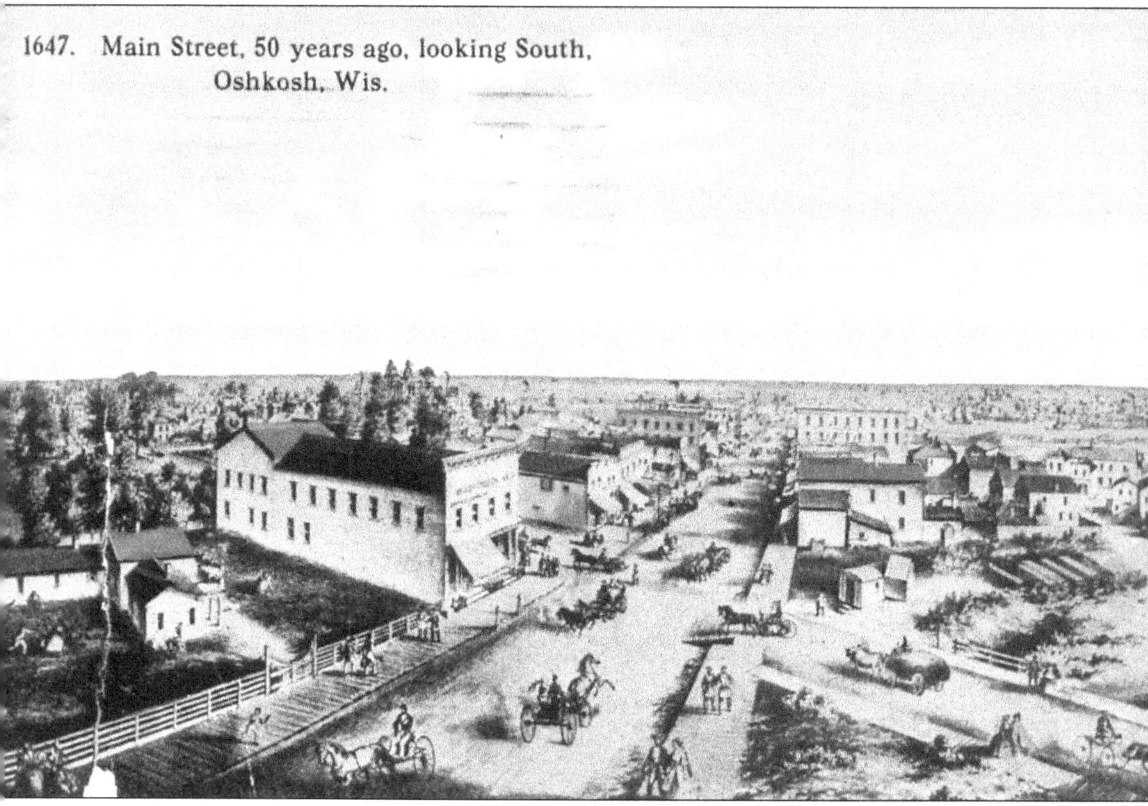

Nostalgia for the past is prominent in this card, postmarked 1911, featuring a view from the 1860s that shows what Main Street looked like before Oshkosh's Great Fire of 1866. After repeated fires in the 1870s, numerous Main Street buildings had to be rebuilt. William Waters designed many of these buildings utilizing stone and brick rather than wood. (Author's collection.)

On the Front Cover: The Continental Clothing Company, pictured on the right side of this postcard, opened in 1891 and produced mostly men's and boys' clothing. Carl Laemmle worked as a manager at this company for seven years before founding Universal Studios in 1912. This card also gives a view of the original Old First National Bank building. Subsequent bank buildings were constructed in 1911 and 1927. (Author's collection.)

On the Back Cover: The "greetings from" postcard is an iconic type. These brightly colored images can paint any American community in an exciting light. This one highlights community icons within the letters. Many of these images are represented as full-size postcards throughout this book. (Author's collection.)

POSTCARD HISTORY SERIES

Oshkosh

Michelle Lokken

ARCADIA
PUBLISHING

ISBN 978-1-4671-0522-4

Published by Arcadia Publishing
Charleston, South Carolina

Library of Congress Control Number: 2020934423

For all general information contact Arcadia Publishing at:
Telephone 843-853-2070
Fax 843-853-0044
E-mail sales@arcadiapublishing.com
For customer service and orders:
Toll-Free 1-888-313-2665

Visit us on the Internet at www.arcadiapublishing.com

To my mother, my number-one supporter in all realms of my life and keeper of all things precious.

Contents

Acknowledgments

I want to thank the many people who helped with and contributed to this book; most of all, the board members of the Winnebago County Historical and Archaeological Society for allowing me to use the donated portion of my grandfather's collection. I especially want to thank board members Austin Frederick and Randy Domer. The idea of publishing a book was intimidating and seemed out of reach for me as a college student. It was immensely inspiring to learn that Austin had published a book about his hometown, Markesan, when he was a University of Wisconsin (UW) Oshkosh history student. I want to thank him for his support with the beginning phases of this project. I also want to thank Randy for his support and for getting me in touch with other postcard collectors.

Thank you to Ron Metz for allowing me to use parts of his extensive Oshkosh postcard collection for this book. It was a pleasure to visit with him, considering he knew my grandfather. Both men were members of the Winnebago County Historical and Archeological Society. I also want to thank Tristan Huss, my coworker at the Paine Art Center & Gardens, for providing additional postcards.

Thank you to Dr. Christine Roth at UW Oshkosh. Her classes over the years have helped me grow as a writer. Dr. Roth challenged me to consider the cultural history behind postcards and to see them as more than just images. Her Oshkosh history–themed advanced composition class was the jump start I needed to embark on this project.

Thank you to Pam Gumz and Joan Kaeding at the Oshkosh Public Library. They pulled endless amounts of material from the local history files for me. I especially want to thank Joan. She is a local history expert who helped me solve any local history mystery that I came across.

Thank you to my grandfather, the late Harold Helm, for his love of history. Although he passed away before I was born, my grandfather has helped me know and appreciate the history of Oshkosh. (See page 126.)

Thank you to my family, and especially my mother, Nancy Lokken. This book would not have been possible without her. She has meticulously kept up and organized her father's postcard collection and documents about our family history. Throughout this project, my mother was there every step of the way editing and proofing my drafts. Her guidance helped make me the best writer I could be. I can never thank her enough.

INTRODUCTION

Oshkosh is one of a kind. The city was named after Menominee chief Oshkosh, who lived from 1795 to 1858. However, it did not always go by that name. When early settlers came to the area, the north side of the river was referred to as Athens, and the south side was loosely known as Brooklyn. The community needed to establish a post office, and in order to do so, it needed to select a name. In 1839, a group of citizens met in George Wright's log cabin to make this decision. Suggestions included Athens, Fairfield, Stanford, Osceola, and Oshkosh. The old-time residents of French descent, led by Robert Grignon, were convinced that the area should be named after Chief Oshkosh. They won the vote, and Oshkosh was born. It was incorporated as a city in 1853. The postcards in this book show a few examples of Oshkosh taking advantage of its unique name. Oshkosh Brewing Company's flagship product was Chief Oshkosh Beer. In the garment industry, OshKosh B'Gosh overalls made the city's name famous worldwide.

This collection of postcards provides a glimpse of what Oshkosh was like in the early 20th century. However, Oshkosh's history goes back much further. Before the city was established, the area was occupied mostly by the Menominee and Winnebago (Ho-Chunk) peoples. Jean Nicolet was the first European to come through the Fox River Valley in 1634. The fur trade shaped initial interactions between the area's native people, the Europeans, and later, westward-moving Americans. In the early 19th century, pioneers further settled the Oshkosh area. In 1818, Augustin Grignon established the area's first trading post on Lake Butte des Morts. Webster Stanley is said to be Oshkosh's first settler, arriving in 1836. Throughout the rest of the 19th century, Oshkosh continued to grow and develop. Lumber became the city's main industry. By the end of the 19th century, Oshkosh earned the nickname "Sawdust City." This book will show Oshkosh as a developing and thriving city in the early 20th century, still connected to its early roots.

Postcards were a revolutionary media in America, and they have obvious connections to our current popular media. Postcards are still relevant today. We continue to buy them just for the simple pleasure of owning them. Postcards are most often associated with travel and tourism. When a friend goes off on a trip to a new and exciting place, we say "send me a postcard." Postcard images encompassed more than just large metropolitan areas. Cities all across America, like Oshkosh, produced their own postcards. Today, it is hard to imagine someone buying an Oshkosh postcard as a souvenir or sending it off to a friend. Years ago, however, postcards were an American cultural phenomenon. They served as souvenirs, collectibles, a means of communication, or even a way to share photographs. The backs of postcards served as an early form of quick correspondence, similar to today's texting. Postcards also offered opportunities to share photographs with friends, similar to current photo-sharing apps like Instagram. People could make their own real-photo postcards by having their photographs developed onto blank postcards and sending them off to friends. Postcards are multi-faceted items that continue to have cultural significance.

Postcards gained popularity in the early 20th century due to modifications in US Postal Service regulations. Originally, the Postal Service charged higher rates for postcards that it did not produce. Additionally, there was no space provided for correspondence on the back. Then, a couple significant changes happened. The price gap between government postcards and private mailing cards closed in 1901, and the backs of postcards became divided in 1907. The divided back provided room for a message and was the main contributor to the increased popularity of postcards. The period of 1907–1915 is commonly referred to as the "Golden Age of Postcards." At this time, millions of postcards were sent in the mail each year, but even more were never sent, as Americans were happy just to keep and collect them. Creating postcard albums was an inexpensive and fun pastime for many people. Cities all across America, like Oshkosh, were feeding the craze and producing postcards of their own communities.

Many of the Oshkosh postcards presented in this book are from the golden age. The majority come from the collection of Harold E. Helm, my maternal grandfather. Harold was a third-generation Oshkosh resident who enjoyed collecting coins and Oshkosh memorabilia. He also had an extensive collection of Oshkosh postcards. After he passed away in 1994, most of his collection was donated to the Winnebago County Historical and Archaeological Society (WCHAS). My mother, Nancy Lokken, thought it fitting to donate most of the postcards to a society her father had been a member of for many years. A portion of Harold's collection was retained. My mother kept a variety of cards, including some that were addressed to Mildred Mackie, his mother. Mildred was a young girl during the Golden Age of Postcards. The collection includes cards received from her friends and relatives. Interestingly, many of the postcards that Mildred received were from friends in town. This collection is uniquely Oshkosh and features cards sent between Oshkosh residents. The importance and value of these postcards have stood the test of time. Most of the cards are over 100 years old. They have passed from my great-grandmother to my grandfather to my mother and then to me.

Postcards were an American cultural phenomenon that touched and represented all communities. For people connected to Oshkosh and those trying to understand this community, these postcards are valuable historical records that illustrate what Oshkosh used to be. Each postcard picture reveals a unique story of Oshkosh's past by showing the places that mattered within the community. A picture can be worth a thousand words, but a postcard collection is worth even more. This collection of vintage Oshkosh postcards has countless words for the city many of us call home.

One

Oshkosh Views

Oshkosh made its mark on Wisconsin's map long ago. From the time of statehood to the year 1900, Oshkosh was the second-largest city in Wisconsin. Its second-city status is captured in this chapter, which features two popular postcard types that give an overarching view of the city. Bird's-eye views and street-view postcards showcase Oshkosh's geographic and urban landscape. Bird's-eye views are essentially artistic drawings that show an aerial view of a community. Although the perspective was somewhat distorted, bird's-eye views were popular in the late 19th century. They made a community look larger and more prosperous than it really was. The craze started with full-size maps but soon expanded to postcards. Actual aerial photography became possible in the 1920s. Soon after, aerial photographs found their way onto postcards, as will be seen in this chapter. These aerial photographs provide an accurate idea of Oshkosh's landscape in the past and depict the city as it really was.

On a smaller scale, street views capture the essence of a bustling community. Oshkosh's Main Street was the hub of commerce in the early 20th century, but it was not always Oshkosh's main street. Modern-day Algoma Boulevard was Oshkosh's first Main Street. The current downtown Main Street was granted its name in 1855 due to the business district growing there. With constantly changing businesses on Main, street-view postcards can tell infinite stories of Oshkosh's past life. Aside from businesses, electric streetcars are also part of the typical Main Street postcard. Streetcars ran throughout Oshkosh and could essentially provide a tour of the city. The postcards in this chapter attempt to do the same, showcasing views of other prominent streets, including Oregon Street, Algoma Boulevard, High Avenue, and Washington Avenue. Although the views of the city are vastly different today, Main Street in Oshkosh still holds much of the same charm it did in the early 20th century.

This postcard encapsulates the idea of a bird's-eye view. Oshkosh is very pronounced on this card compared to other similar-sized cities in the region like Appleton. Some Oshkosh sites are marked, including Electric Park, Northern Hospital, and Indian Point. (Author's collection.)

Oshkosh's location on Lake Winnebago and the Fox River was central to its development as a city and its growth in the lumber industry. This postcard provides a view of the entire Lake Winnebago region and makes note of other cities in the Fox Valley. (Courtesy of WCHAS.)

Taken in the 1950s, this aerial view of the Fox River in Oshkosh shows the majority of the city's bridges. The second bridge from the top is the Soo Line Railroad Bridge. This bridge was built in 1904 and was serviced until its removal in 1999. After this, Oshkosh's rail service was consolidated through the Chicago & North Western Railroad Bridge, which is shown at the bottom of the postcard. (Courtesy of WCHAS.)

This aerial shot from the late 1960s shows the Pioneer Inn and Marina. Construction of this hotel changed the landscape of Oshkosh's waterfront. Rubble from the Athearn Hotel, which was razed in 1964, was used as fill to build up Ki Ni Island for the construction of the Pioneer Inn in 1965. The marina, to the left of the inn, could hold up to 250 boats. (Courtesy of WCHAS.)

In the 1920s, with the dawn of aerial photography, images like this overtook traditional bird's-eye views. This one shows the Fox River feeding into Lake Winnebago. The Main Street Bridge and former Chicago & North Western Railroad Bridge are in the foreground. Oshkosh's south side was full of industry. Part of the Morgan Company factory can be seen at lower right. (Courtesy of WCHAS.)

This view from the 1920s focuses on the intersection of Main Street and Church Avenue. The postcard directly overlooks the corner turret of the building that is currently occupied by Salon Mode. The businesses along the right side of Main Street were all rebuilt after the fourth Great Fire of 1874. Many of these structures are still present today. (Courtesy of WCHAS.)

In this view overlooking the southeast part of Oshkosh's downtown, the Fox River can be seen in the background. Oshkosh City Hall, with its prominent tower, is on the left. City hall was on the northwest corner of State and Otter Streets and stood until 1964. (Courtesy of WCHAS.)

Likely from the late 1930s, this postcard looks north up Main Street. Like today, businesses on Main Street are always changing. A Piggly Wiggly sign is visible on the right, on the second building from the bottom. It opened in 1938 and was considered the largest Piggly Wiggly in the state at the time. (Courtesy of WCHAS.)

Main Street's electric streetcars are featured on this 1914 postcard. Starting in 1882, Oshkosh had animal-powered streetcars. Electrified lines started in 1896. With nearly 32 miles' worth of routes in Oshkosh, electric streetcars were a common method of transportation. They remained popular until the 1920s and were gradually replaced with motor buses. Streetcar service in Oshkosh officially ended in 1930. (Author's collection.)

On the right is the First National Bank building on the corner of Main Street and Washington Avenue. This bank rebuilt multiple times at the same location. This postcard features the second building, which was constructed in 1911 and stood until 1927, when a new eight-story bank was built. The 1927 building still stands and can be seen in later postcards. (Courtesy of WCHAS.)

Both of these cards are Main Street views looking north from approximately Washington Avenue. They feature the street scene during the day and at night. Both the view and the pedestrians are exactly the same on both. Typically, the "nighttime" scene was adapted from a photograph taken in broad daylight. Vintage postcards are more an adaptable artistic medium than a picture-perfect depiction of a location. The Lyric Theatre, whose sign is visible on the right, showed motion pictures and sold tickets for only 5¢. (Both, courtesy of WCHAS.)

This view of Main Street looks west down High Avenue. The intersection is marked with two banks. Commercial National Bank is on the left, and City National Bank is on the right. The building at the end of High Avenue is the Athearn Hotel, which was completed in 1891. George Athearn, the owner, was determined that the hotel be constructed purely from Oshkosh products. (Courtesy of WCHAS.)

This is a similar view as the previous postcard, but one block back. Two of Oshkosh's major hotels can be seen. The Athearn is at the end of the street, and the Tremont is on the right. The Tremont Hotel was on the corner of Waugoo Avenue and State Street. (Author's collection.)

The Oshkosh Theater was located where Kitz and Pfeil True Value Hardware is today. The theater opened in the late 1920s, toward the end of the silent-film era. It had its own organ to add sound effects to silent films. When this image was created, the theater was showing the 1926 drama *Fire Brigade*. The view is looking south down Main Street from approximately Church Avenue. (Author's collection.)

This view from the 1930s looks north up Main Street from High Avenue. The left side is lined with shops, but today, that area is green space. The urban park Opera House Square was part of the city's downtown revitalization efforts and was completed in 2002. (Author's collection.)

The Raulf Hotel can be seen in the background of this 1930s Main Street view. This hotel was originally home to the Fischer Theatre, later renamed the Strand Theater. In 1928, the Strand was the first theater in Oshkosh that had sound projection and could play "talkies." (Courtesy of WCHAS.)

This night view of Main Street in the 1940s looks north from Waugoo Avenue. Richman Brothers Clothing Company can be seen on the right. Farther back is the First National Bank building, which still stands today. (Courtesy of WCHAS.)

This 1960s view looks north up Main Street. The Time Theatre's marquee is on the left. Of all of Oshkosh's downtown movie theatres, the Time is the only one still open today. The building was home to multiple theaters in the early 20th century but became the Time Theatre in 1939. (Author's collection.)

The S.S. Kresge Company dime store can be seen on the left side of this postcard. In the past, shopping trips were daylong events, and S.S. Kresge had a variety of products. It was the largest discount retailer of its time and was eventually renamed Kmart in 1977. (Author's collection.)

Oregon Street was essentially Oshkosh's second main street, with its own business district including retailers, grocery stores, and a bank. Its location was more convenient for south side residents. This view depicts the area at night looking south from Eighth Avenue. A billboard for Stars Clothing House is on the right. (Author's collection.)

Oregon Street and Ninth Avenue were part of the city's electric streetcar routes. Whitley and Weeks Department Store is on the left. The State Bank of Oshkosh is on the right. Both buildings still stand today. (Author's collection.)

Washington Street is a combination of neoclassical buildings, both public and private, and residential homes. The western end has the public library, the post office, the Masonic temple, and the Wisconsin National Life Insurance Building. The eastern end has elaborate Victorian houses. This view shows the residential area. Washington Street was included in the city's electric streetcar routes. (Courtesy of WCHAS.)

This scenic postcard, showing tree-lined Algoma Boulevard, is postmarked 1912. It was addressed to Mildred Mackie, the author's great-grandmother, who was visiting relatives in Milwaukee. Mildred's sister, Sylvia, wrote to tell her about the spring snow in Oshkosh. (Author's collection.)

Church Street (now Avenue) has a very literal name, since the north side of the street has historically been lined with churches. The First Presbyterian Church is on the left. This site was originally a Methodist church. In 1875, Oshkosh Presbyterians bought the building, and later built their own church in 1893. (Courtesy of WCHAS.)

In the early 20th century, Oshkosh residents used rural country roads like this to access Lake Butte des Morts. The end of Oakwood Road was a popular destination for picnics and camping. When this card was produced around 1915, the city of Oshkosh essentially ended at Eagle Road, west of the Fox River. (Courtesy of WCHAS.)

Two

BUILDINGS

Postcards of Oshkosh buildings represent much more than the buildings themselves; they represent the organizations and people that work within them. Oshkosh is unique in regard to its buildings and architecture. The majority of the city's historic buildings were designed by William Waters. His buildings can be seen throughout the state of Wisconsin, but Oshkosh has the largest concentration of his work. Buildings designed by Waters are featured in countless postcards of Oshkosh.

William Waters was born in New York in 1843. He studied at the Rensselaer Polytechnic Institute in Troy, New York, and then moved to Oshkosh in 1867 at the age of 24. There was plenty of work and opportunity for Waters in Oshkosh. The city experienced five major fires between 1859 and 1875. Known as "Sawdust City" and considered to be the lumber capital of the world, it is not a surprise that the city endured fires. Abundant amounts of sawdust and lumber were major fire hazards. The city was in constant need of rebuilding. Waters moved to Oshkosh just after the second Great Fire of 1866. He redesigned many of the city's buildings in stone. The first was St. Peter's Catholic Church in 1867. Over the course of his 50-year career, Waters designed over 150 buildings in the Oshkosh area. His portfolio includes schools, churches, hospitals, banks, public buildings, commercial buildings, and private residences. If a historic building in Oshkosh was not designed by William Waters, it was likely designed by his protégé Henry Auler, who designed many of the historic buildings on Washington Avenue. These two men, especially Waters, have left an immense mark on Oshkosh. Their work has stood the test of time and still makes up a large part of Oshkosh's architectural landscape today.

Built entirely of cream city brick in a Romanesque Revival architectural style, the Grand Opera House is perhaps one of William Waters's most iconic designs. Waters was chosen as the architect for the project after the Business Men's Association of Oshkosh ran a successful subscription drive to raise the necessary $30,000 in capital stock for the project. This group felt that Oshkosh, Wisconsin's second-largest city, needed a suitable theater and entertainment center. The Grand opened in 1883 and was considered one of the finest theaters in the Midwest. The interior was decorated with frescos by Oshkosh artist Frank J. Waldo. Adam Bell and Edwin Cole were the contractors for the interior woodwork. The lavish interior helped the opera house attract acts with national reputations. Much later, in the 1950s, the Grand showed only motion pictures. The building fell into disrepair in the 1970s, and at its lowest point operated as an X-rated movie theater. Major restoration efforts in the 1980s brought the Grand back to its original condition and prestige. (Author's collection.)

Diagonally across from the Grand Opera House, the Athearn Hotel was also a William Waters design. The hotel was the vision of George Athearn, who wanted to build a premier hotel completely sourced from Oshkosh products. Oshkosh citizens helped fund the hotel through a subscription drive. Completed in 1891, the Athearn boasted 75 rooms and two luxurious dining halls. (Courtesy of WCHAS.)

The Tremont House, on the corner of State Street and Waugoo Avenue, opened in 1865. Following the Great Fire of 1875, William Waters redesigned the ruined hotel. The new structure is pictured here. This is an example of an undivided-back postcard, with the message on the front. Before 1907, only the address was permitted on the back. (Author's collection.)

The Oshkosh Public Library is a prime example of neoclassical architecture. William Waters's design included Ionic columns and a 46-foot dome. Construction began in 1899, and the library opened in 1900. The first floor was the actual library, while the second floor housed a lecture room and a museum from 1905 to 1924. The library was massively expanded in 1993 to better serve the community. (Author's collection.)

William Waters designed an English Tudor Revival–style home for Edgar and Mary Jewell Sawyer. Constructed between 1908 and 1909, the interior of this 35-room home was decorated by Tiffany Studios. As a result of Mary's unexpected passing in 1909, Edgar did not occupy the home much and decided to donate it to the city in 1922. The city opened it as the Oshkosh Public Museum in 1924. (Author's collection.)

The Old Ladies Home on North Main Street was a William Waters design completed in 1901. The home was run by the Ladies Benevolent Society and served elderly and impoverished women until 1974. The society was founded just before the Civil War, making it one of the state's oldest philanthropic organizations. The society aided families of Civil War soldiers and continued to aid the impoverished after the war. (Author's collection.)

The *Oshkosh Daily Northwestern* dates to 1861. This postcard shows the newspaper's new building, constructed in 1930 on the corner of State Street and Waugoo Avenue. The back of the postcard describes the *Northwestern* as "Wisconsin's Greatest Family Newspaper." In the 1930s, when this postcard was made, the paper's circulation was 16,250. (Courtesy of WCHAS.)

The Fraternal Reserve Association (FRA) was founded in 1902 and served the area as a fraternal organization and an insurance provider. The Fraternal Reserve building, completed in 1914, was designed by Henry Auler, a protégé of William Waters. When the FRA merged with Equitable Fraternal Union of Neenah in 1930, the offices moved to Neenah. The building is currently used as apartments. (Author's collection.)

The Wisconsin National Life Insurance Company was established in 1908. It was Wisconsin's first incorporated reserve stock life insurance company. This building was a Henry Auler design, constructed in 1927. It is a prime example of Neoclassical Greek Revival architecture with its use of Corinthian columns and an ornate frieze with griffins, scrolls, and lion heads. The company occupied this building until it was sold in 1993. (Author's collection.)

Oshkosh Lodge No. 27, Free and Accepted Masons, was designed by Henry Auler and completed in 1924. Masonry in Oshkosh dates to 1849. Lodge No. 27 previously had a temple on Main Street next to the National Bank building. With growing membership during the early 1900s, a new location and a larger building became necessary. The Oshkosh Masons still occupy this temple. (Author's collection.)

Another Henry Auler design is the Eagles clubhouse on Washington Avenue. This English Tudor Revival–style building opened in 1928 as the home for Oshkosh's Fraternal Order of the Eagles. Their clubhouse included a ballroom, a stage, and a 10-lane bowling alley. The building was renovated and opened as an upscale event venue called the Howard in 2018. (Author's collection.)

The Oshkosh chapter of the Benevolent and Protective Order of the Elks was chartered in 1885. The Elks built their clubhouse on Jefferson Street in 1913. This building no longer stands. The city bought the site in 1977 to build a parking lot for Main Street businesses. The Oshkosh Elks Club No. 292 is active today and meets on West Fernau Avenue. (Courtesy of WCHAS.)

This building on Court Street was home to Lodge No. 282 of the Loyal Order of Moose. The lodge was founded in 1910 and bought this building from another fraternal organization called the Sons of Herrmann. The building was sold to the Oshkosh Trades and Labor Council in 1939. Today, it is privately owned. (Courtesy of WCHAS.)

The Oshkosh Yacht Club existed for nearly 35 years without its own clubhouse. In 1903, the club's 600 members funded the construction of a clubhouse. William Waters sold his lakefront property to the club and designed the building. The project moved very quickly. After Waters's home was razed, the clubhouse was completed in only three months. (Author's collection.)

The Oshkosh Country Club started as the Algoma Club in 1899 and was located at the former Lakeshore Municipal Golf Course site. Philetus Sawyer was the club's first president. In 1917, the club moved to the Weyerhorst Farm site on the south side of town and renamed itself the Oshkosh Country Club. This postcard shows the club's new south side location. (Courtesy of WCHAS.)

As Wisconsin's second city, Oshkosh wanted an elegant structure to represent itself. William Waters designed Oshkosh's first city hall in a Romanesque style with red brick. On the corner of Otter and State Streets, the building served the city from 1888 to 1964. The city's major departments were housed here, along with the municipal court and jail. The current city hall is pictured later in this chapter. (Author's collection.)

The State Street Fire Truck House, more simply known as the "Truck House," was designed by William Waters and built in 1889. The Truck House was the home base for the city's hook and ladder trucks and fire engines. This building was purposely built with red brick to correspond with city hall, which was just down the street. (Author's collection.)

Oshkosh's post office was established in 1840 but did not have a formal location until 1890. The post office stood on the corner of Washington and Jefferson Avenues. The upper floors were for federal use, housing US Circuit Court rooms and offices for the Internal Revenue Service. Although the post office looks similar to city hall, it is not a Waters design. This building was razed in 1939. (Author's collection.)

Oshkosh outgrew its first post office. A new building was constructed in the late 1920s and opened for use in 1931. Unlike most buildings on Washington Avenue, this was not a Henry Auler design. It is credited to James A. Wetmore, who worked for the US Treasury Department as acting supervising architect. Like the first post office, the upper floors housed federal offices. (Author's collection.)

The founding of Winnebago County dates to 1840. Oshkosh was named the county seat, and a small wooden courthouse was completed in 1849. This postcard shows the county's second courthouse. It originally had a dome. In 1872, the dome was replaced with a tower, as pictured. The courthouse was further renovated in the 1870s. William Waters designed the additional wings off the central building. (Courtesy of WCHAS.)

Winnebago County's current courthouse was built in 1937. (The second was razed in 1939.) The new limestone structure features sculptures around entrances and on window spandrels. The sculptures on the main entrance depict the functions of the courthouse, whereas the spandrels and other entrances feature symbols of home life, adventure, and industry. The work was completed by Chicago sculptors Alfonso Iannelli and Ruth Blackwell. (Courtesy of WCHAS.)

Smith School was named after John Smith, one of Oshkosh's earliest settlers. Smith arrived in Oshkosh in 1845 and built a wooden schoolhouse on his property in 1866. He taught at the school and then donated it to the city. The building pictured here was designed by William Waters and opened in 1896. This original building served students until Smith School closed in 2019. (Courtesy of WCHAS.)

Merrill was Oshkosh's 10th Ward School. The structure pictured here was built in 1900 and named to commemorate the unexpected passing of Oshkosh mayor James H. Merrill. Originally, Merrill was an elementary school. The current building was constructed in 1932 and includes both elementary and middle school sections. (Courtesy of WCHAS.)

Lincoln School was on the corner of Algoma Boulevard and Wisconsin Avenue. This site was previously Oshkosh's first cemetery, Locust Grove. The first school was built in 1859, after all the graves had been relocated to Riverside Cemetery. The structure pictured here was a William Waters design built in 1888. It was renamed Lincoln School in 1910. Today, the site serves as the UW Oshkosh Children's Learning and Care Center. (Courtesy of WCHAS.)

The original South Park Elementary School (pictured) was built in 1904. Today's structure opened in 1940 as an elementary and junior high school. The 1940 South Park school was one of the first buildings in Oshkosh to have an indoor swimming pool. South Park Elementary was discontinued in 1971. The building has served exclusively as a middle school since. (Author's collection.)

Oshkosh's original 1868 high school was destroyed by fire in 1901. This prompted the construction of a new high school (above) in 1903. It could accommodate 550 students but was quickly outgrown. In response, Orville Beach Manual Training School, pictured on the right below, was built in 1911. Orville Beach was a local businessman whose estate was donated to create a school dedicated to industrial arts. The manual training school was designed by William Waters. However, a bigger high school building was still needed. Waters and Henry Auler designed a new Oshkosh High School in 1914. The new building served as the area's high school until 1961, when Oshkosh West opened. Currently, the high school building is Oshkosh City Hall. (Both, author's collection.)

The first county farm facility opened in 1871. Also known as poor farms, these facilities were often places to house the poor or mentally ill. The original building was in dire condition by 1906. This postcard shows the building that William Waters designed to replace the previous facility. All structures were razed in 1968, and the site is now Winnebago County Community Park. (Courtesy of WCHAS.)

The Winnebago County Asylum was established in reaction to legislation in the 1880s that called for a new system of care for mental illness. Designed by William Waters and constructed in 1893, the asylum lightened the load on the county farm. Since 1957, this institution has changed its name and mission greatly. Today, it is Park View Health Center nursing home. (Author's collection.)

The city of Oshkosh was selected as the second location for a state mental institute. The Northern State Hospital could accommodate up to 500 patients and admitted its first in 1873. This William Waters design was based on the Kirkbride plan. The center part was for administration, with the patient wings extending out. The original building was razed in 1969. (Courtesy of WCHAS.)

The Northern Hospital for the Insane changed its name and mission over the years. This card is postmarked 1910 and refers to the Northern Hospital as "State Hospital." In 1935, the institution was officially renamed Winnebago State Hospital. In 1973, the name changed again to the Winnebago Mental Health Institute, as it is known today. (Courtesy of WCHAS.)

Alexian Brothers Hospital is regarded as Oshkosh's first regular hospital. It opened in 1879 in a remodeled home on Jackson Street. The Alexian Brothers were part of a Catholic institute dedicated to helping the sick but limiting their services to men. After helping Chicago industrial workers, they sought to help another community with similar dire industrial conditions. Oshkosh was the perfect candidate as a cheap labor town. This postcard shows the second Alexian Brothers Hospital, which was constructed on the same site in 1884. The hospital also operated as a sanitarium and later as a retirement home. At the end of its life, the hospital building ironically served as a female dormitory for UW Oshkosh, called East Hall during the late 1960s. The building was razed in 1971. Today, the site is East Hall Park, consisting of athletic fields for UW Oshkosh. (Courtesy of WCHAS.)

St. Mary's Hospital opened in 1891 and was part of St. Mary's Church. The Sisterhood of the Sorrowful Mother ran the hospital. In 1895, Oshkosh's former mayor and architect Ephraim E. Stevens designed this much larger facility. On the corner of Boyd Street and Merritt Avenue, it could house up to 75 patients. It functioned as a hospital until 1934. (Courtesy of WCHAS.)

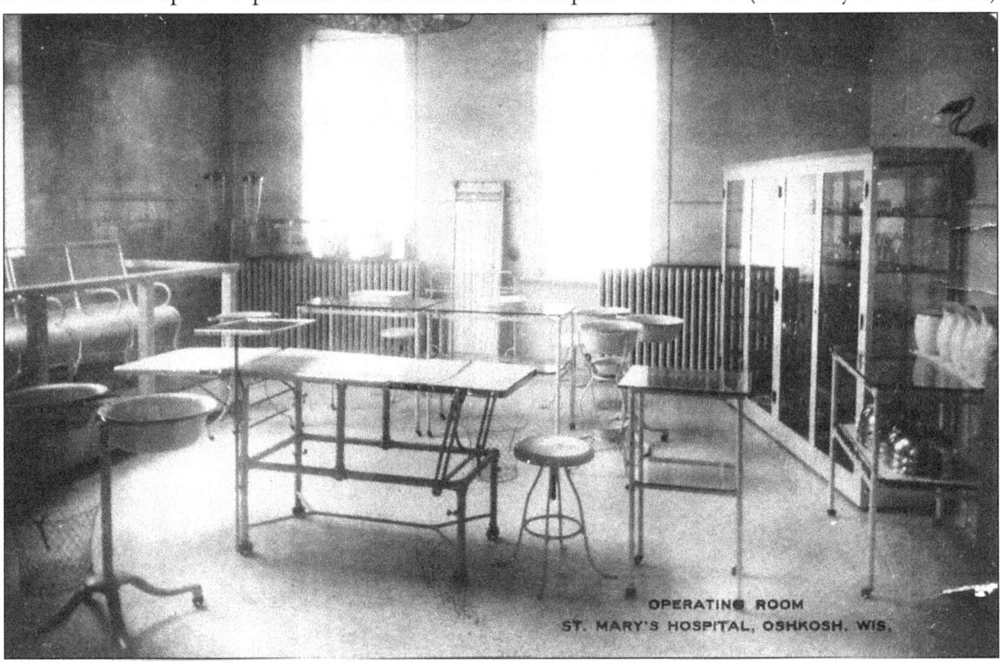

Postmarked 1908, this postcard of an operating room at St. Mary's Hospital gives an idea as to what medical technology was like at the time. A tool cabinet can be seen on the right. The row of chairs on the left was likely for spectators. Operating theaters, where spectators could watch operations, existed throughout the 19th and early 20th centuries. (Courtesy of Ron Metz.)

Lakeside Sanitarium was organized by Dr. Michael E. Corbett in 1887. It originally operated out of a home on the corner of Washington Avenue and Hazel Street. In 1906, Dr. Corbett established the city's first nursing school in connection with Lakeside Sanitarium. The building pictured here was a William Waters design, built in 1912–1913 on Hazel Street. The hospital was considered fireproof and had an automatic elevator. (Courtesy of WCHAS.)

This postcard features the same building with a different name. Lakeside Sanitarium was renamed Mercy Hospital in 1918 when the Sisters of the Sorrowful Mother, who ran St. Mary's Hospital, took ownership. The sisters used both buildings as Mercy Hospital until 1934. (Courtesy of Ron Metz.)

Mercy Hospital went through expansion projects to keep up with Oshkosh's growth. In 1922 and 1938, a north and south wing were added, respectively. When this postcard was produced in the 1940s, patient capacity was 215. Mercy continued to expand and outgrew this facility. In 2000, an entirely new hospital was built on Oakwood Road. The building on Hazel Street is now a retirement community and apartments. (Courtesy of Ron Metz.)

When Lakeside Sanitarium became Mercy Hospital in 1918, the school was renamed Mercy Hospital School of Nursing. This postcard shows the facility that was created for the school in 1931. Mercy was a diploma school and offered on-the-job training. Diploma schools were being phased out in the 1980s, and the school closed in 1982. Oshkosh's nursing legacy continues with UW Oshkosh's nursing program. (Courtesy of WCHAS.)

First Congregational Church was organized in 1849. The building in the foreground was designed by William Waters and completed in 1912. The 170-foot spire in the background is the previous church building, which Waters designed in 1873. Waters purposely designed the new church in a Gothic style to correspond with the old church, which continued to be used as a fellowship hall. (Courtesy of WCHAS.)

Trinity Episcopal Church's congregation dates to 1850. The pictured church is an 1887 William Waters design. Local attorney Charles Barber commissioned Tiffany Studios of New York to create a window in memory of his wife, Sarah "Daisy" Barber. The 13-foot rose window depicts the Angel of Prayer. The angel's face closely resembles Daisy. In 2006, the window underwent a major restoration. (Author's collection.)

Oshkosh's Baptist church was organized in 1854. The first two buildings occupied by the congregation were destroyed by fire in 1875 and 1901. J.M. Deal was the leading architect of this building. Construction started in 1901, and the church opened in 1902. This building still stands and is a fine example of neoclassical architecture. (Courtesy of WCHAS.)

Founded in 1887, Christ Lutheran Church had a small building on Church Avenue. It was moved to create room for the church pictured here. This church served as the main building from 1903 until 1920. Then, like before, the 1903 church was moved when a new structure was built. Today, this building serves as the parish center for Calvary SonRise Oshkosh. (Courtesy of WCHAS.)

Beginning in 1872, Oshkosh Presbyterians originally met in a church on Jefferson Street. The congregation moved to Church Avenue in 1875 following a trade with the local Methodist church. The Presbyterians exchanged their Jefferson Street church plus $6,000 for the Methodist's building. The church pictured here was the result of a rebuild in 1893. It still stands as First Presbyterian. (Courtesy of WCHAS.)

Algoma Methodist Church was established in 1872. The congregation originally met in a hall above a Paine Lumber Company paint shop. The Romanesque-style church pictured here was designed by William Waters and completed in 1893. Some of Oshkosh's prominent families belonged to this church, including the Paines, Sawyers, and McMillens. Today, it is home to the largest permanently displayed nativity collection in the world. (Author's collection.)

Established in 1848, St. Peter's Catholic Church was Oshkosh's first Catholic church. The building pictured here was William Waters's first Oshkosh commission. The foundation was laid in 1867, but the project was not completed until 1880. This building served the congregation until 1954, when a new church was built. The 1954 structure stands today as the St. Peter's site of Most Blessed Sacrament Parish. (Courtesy of WCHAS.)

St. Peter's High School, dedicated in 1914, was also a William Waters design. The school closed in 1959 but the building still stands today. It serves as the office building for Most Blessed Sacrament Parish. (Courtesy of WCHAS.)

St. Mary's Church was formed in 1857 as an outgrowth of St. Peter's Catholic Church. With the growing population in Oshkosh, St. Mary's was specifically built to serve German immigrants. The original church was replaced with the elaborate Victorian Gothic cathedral pictured here. The new church was dedicated in 1892 and still stands today as the St. Mary's site of Most Blessed Sacrament Parish. (Courtesy of WCHAS.)

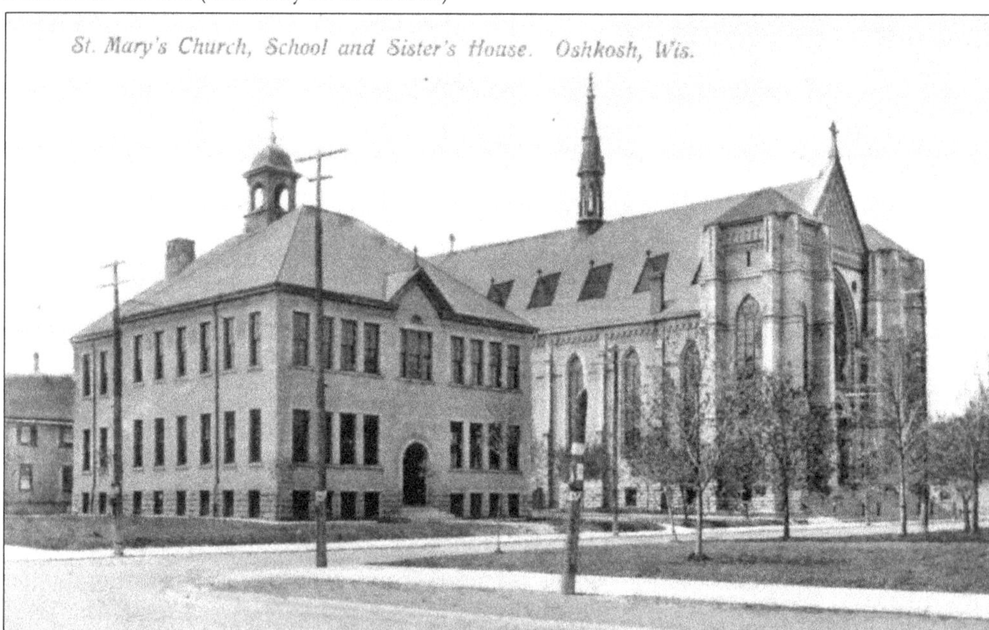

Similar to St. Peter's, St. Mary's had its own school. The school building pictured here was constructed in 1904. In 1925, the school underwent major renovations and additions to accommodate a four-year high school. This building still stands and was previously St. Francis Cabrini Elementary School. (Courtesy of WCHAS.)

Organized in 1868, St. Vincent De Paul's Church first operated out of a wooden building. In 1888, a 145-foot-tall clock tower was added. The building pictured here was constructed in 1914–1915. It still has the original two bells and clock from the previous building. Today, it is home to the St. Vincent Church of St. Jude the Apostle Parish. (Courtesy of WCHAS.)

Sacred Heart Church was formed in 1906 after splitting from St. Vincent's. The church pictured here was built in the same year on the corner of Fifth Avenue and Knapp Street. This church also housed a school. In 1938, a new church was built next to the original, which now serves as a school. This 1938 structure is currently the Sacred Heart Church of St. Jude the Apostle Parish. (Courtesy of WCHAS.)

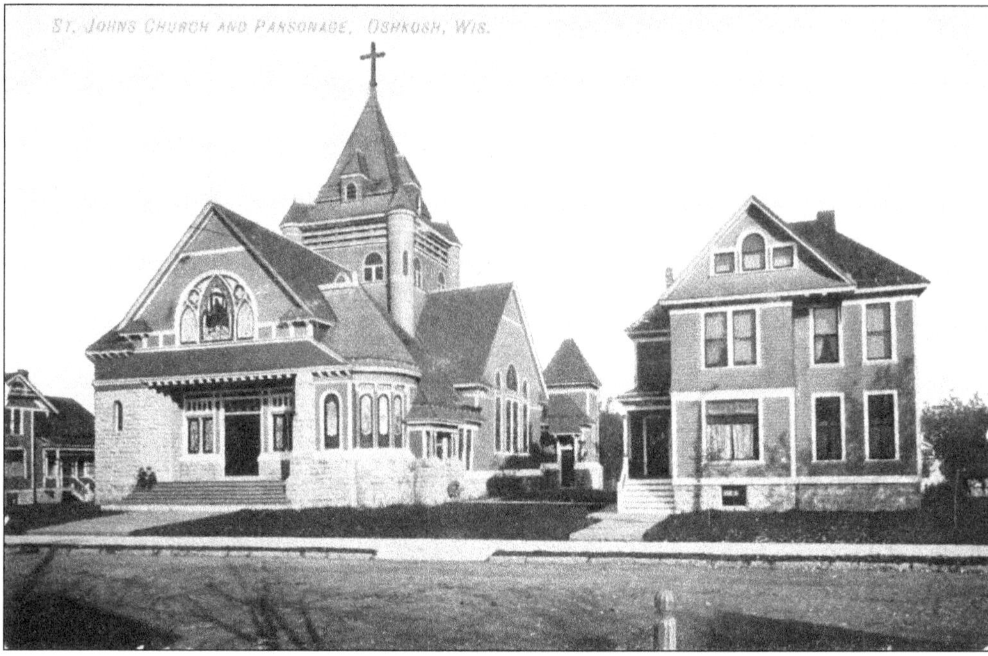

St. John's Catholic Church was established in 1893 when Irish members from St. Vincent's started their own parish. Their building was completed in 1897 on South Park Avenue. St. John's was one of the city's first churches to hold mass in English. In 2008, it merged back into St. Jude the Apostle Parish. Today, this building is home to River of Life Church. (Courtesy of WCHAS.)

Unlike most of the other Catholic schools in Oshkosh, St. John's School was not right next to its parent church. Built in 1909, the school was directly behind the church, on Twelfth Avenue. Today, the building is used as apartments. (Courtesy of WCHAS.)

Three

Industry and Business

Oshkosh's first sawmill opened in 1854. Twenty years later, the city was home to 46 lumber operations, including sawmills, shingle mills, and sash and door factories. Oshkosh earned the nickname "Sawdust City" and was even considered the "Lumber Capitol of the World." During the late 19th and early 20th centuries, major Oshkosh woodworking companies included wood furniture manufacturers like Buckstaff, along with sash door and blind factories like the Paine Lumber Company and Morgan Doors. The postcards in this chapter reflect a time when Oshkosh had fewer but larger sawmills. Scenes of factory buildings on a postcard assert Oshkosh's industrial prominence and could also be used as promotional material. This chapter features part of a collection of Buckstaff company postcards that show the various parts of the lumber industry.

Oshkosh had a diverse economy and excelled in other areas. Most notably, the city built up its name as a brand through OshKosh B'Gosh, the workware turned children's clothes company. Oshkosh was also home to America's largest Diamond Match factory. Oshkosh companies created other products like beer, grass rugs, and motorboat engines. Along with these special products, the city also had a variety of local specialty shops. The gem of Oshkosh retail was Stein's Unique Shop, a fine women's clothing store where the merchandise was elegantly displayed throughout a Victorian mansion. All of these industries and businesses needed financing. Oshkosh was home to multiple banks, which added unique architecture to the city. Economic development helped Oshkosh grow and promote itself as a destination. The city was home to many hotels, most notably the Athearn. Many of the industries and businesses featured in this chapter no longer exist. However, they remain an important part of the city's past. Oshkosh will always have its origins as Sawdust City, but today, it has reinvented itself into "Wisconsin's Event City."

With lumber as its major industry, Oshkosh earned the nickname Sawdust City. The Fox River's connection to the Wolf River gave Oshkosh access to the North Woods. Thousands of lumberjacks worked the woods during the winter. In the spring, log drivers worked the river, sending lumber downstream to Oshkosh. Buckstaff-Edwards Company in Oshkosh produced a series of postcards intended to show the parts of the lumber industry. Each postcard in the series includes Buckstaff's slogan "The Quality Kind." These two show lumberjacks and log drivers hard at work. These efforts in the North Woods are what fueled the lumber companies downriver in Oshkosh. (Both, courtesy of Ron Metz.)

The cook shanty was arguably one of the most important parts of any lumber camp. Although lumberjacks were poorly paid, they were by far some of the best-fed workers. This scene shows a typical logging camp cook shanty. (Courtesy of Ron Metz.)

This postcard shows two workers posing with a team of oxen. Animals like oxen and horses were an immense help during the logging process. After trees were cut down, they would be bundled up and pulled onto a sleigh by a team of oxen. (Courtesy of Ron Metz.)

The Paine Lumber Company was founded in 1853 by Edward L. Paine. When this postcard was produced in the early 1900s, Edward's son George M. Paine served as company president. The mill pictured here was constructed in 1895, during George's tenure. At full capacity, this mill could turn a raw plank into a finished door in 45 seconds. George's son Nathan Paine ran the company from 1917 until he passed away in 1947. Under Nathan's tenure, the company expanded and essentially became a miniature company town, with its own fire station, bank, and housing. The Paine Lumber Company reached its peak in 1929, when it was considered the largest sash, door, and blind factory in the world. Nathan Paine was the last immediate family member to run the company. After its closure in 1983, the majority of Paine Lumber Company's buildings were razed. Today, Fox River Brewing Company resides at the site of the mill. Nearby on Algoma Boulevard is the Paine Art Center & Gardens, which was founded by Nathan Paine. (Courtesy of Ron Metz.)

The large mill building on the left is the only Paine Lumber Company building that still stands. Constructed in 1908, this mill helped Paine grow to be the world's largest manufacturer of door and window sashes. Shortly after the company closed in 1983, this large mill building was converted into condos. (Courtesy of Ron Metz.)

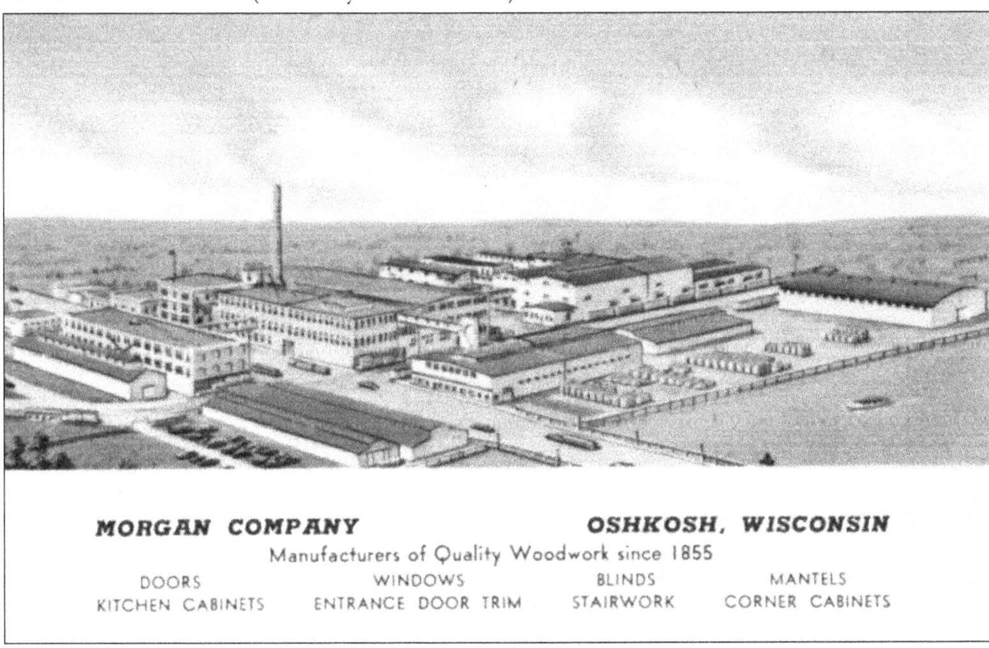

The Morgan Company dates to 1855. It was founded by brothers Richard T. and John R. Morgan. Fire struck the company multiple times. The structures depicted here date to the early 1900s. The Winnebago County Historical and Archeological Society, which provided many of the postcards for this book, operates out of John R. Morgan's 1884 Queen Anne–style home at 234 Church Avenue. (Courtesy of Ron Metz.)

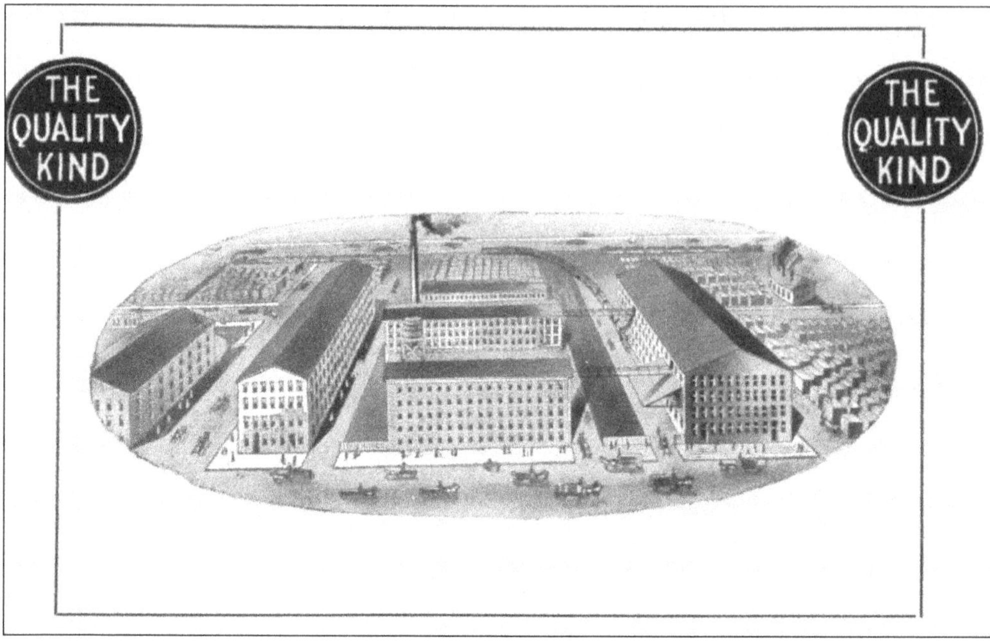

John Buckstaff moved to Oshkosh in 1850 and opened a sawmill with his brothers in 1865. Buckstaff products included caskets and wooden furniture. Their plant was on South Main Street. In 1993, Buckstaff furnished the newly remodeled Oshkosh Public Library. The company's wooden chairs are still used in the library today. Buckstaff closed in 2011 as one of Wisconsin's longest-run family businesses. (Courtesy of Ron Metz.)

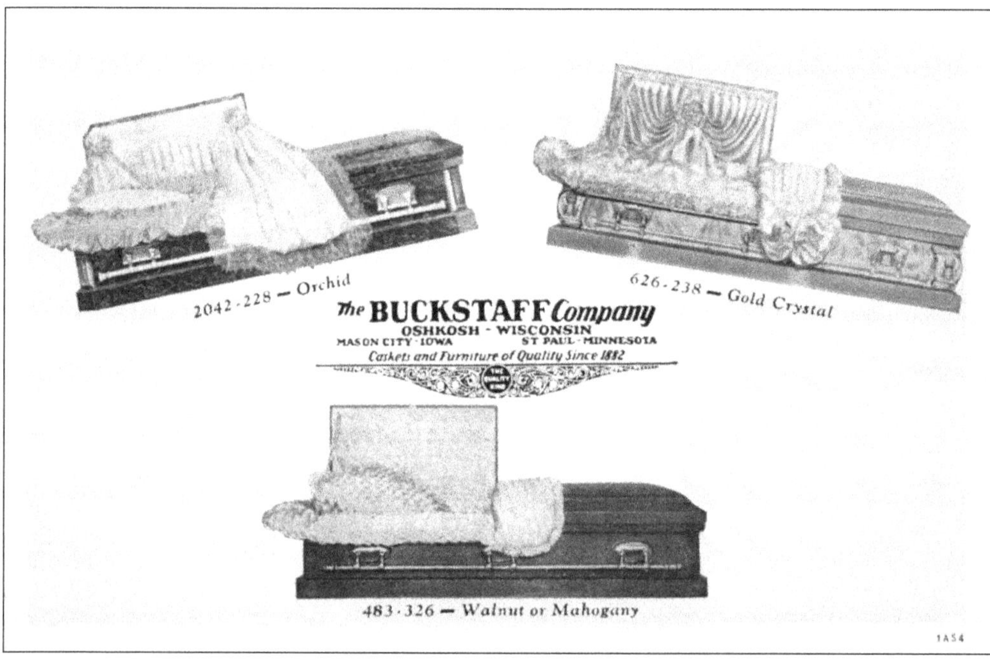

Originally, Buckstaff made caskets. This postcard showcases its different models. A wholesale dealer in undertaker's supplies and goods, the company helped shape the casket industry in the United States. (Courtesy of Ron Metz.)

These two postcards depict Oshkosh's first major railway, the Chicago & North Western. This line was extended from Fond du Lac to Oshkosh in 1859. The resulting connection with Chicago expanded Oshkosh's market, immensely helping its lumber industry. The timing of the railroad's arrival, before the Civil War, also worked out favorably for the city. Lumber from Oshkosh was used to build Union forts. By the time these postcards were produced in the early 1900s, numerous tracks ran through Oshkosh, including the Milwaukee Road, Chicago & North Western, and Wisconsin Central lines. Oshkosh industry benefited from railways, and so did Oshkosh residents. Constructed in 1884, the Chicago & North Western depot operated as a stop on a passenger line to Milwaukee and Chicago until 1971. Although it is in disrepair, the depot still stands today. (Above, courtesy of WCHAS; below, author's collection.)

The Oshkosh Logging Tool Company was founded by Elmer Leach in 1887. The pictured plant building was constructed in 1904 on the south side of the Main Street Bridge. Beginning in 1910, the company diversified and started producing refuse trucks. In 1922, it was renamed Leach Company. Federal Signal Corporation acquired the company in 2002, but the tool business has been operating locally under the name Oshkosh Tools since. (Courtesy of WCHAS.)

Universal Motor Company dates to 1898. Chicagoan E. Homer Fahrney owned a summer home in Oshkosh and was an avid boater. Fahrney built and patented an engine for his boat. He later teamed up with two others and formed Universal Motor Company, which became a major boat engine manufacturer, distributing throughout the United States. This postcard shows the company's Harrison Street location, which still stands. (Courtesy of Ron Metz.)

Diamond Match Company was formed in 1881 as the result of a six-way merger between match companies across the nation. Oshkosh's Star Match Works, founded by James L. Clark in 1868, was part of this merger. Clark's company was highly successful because of a machine he created that made match splints. This work had previously been done by hand. As the postcard notes, Oshkosh had the largest American branch. (Courtesy of Ron Metz.)

Oshkosh's Diamond Match Company was on the corner of Pearl and Osceola Avenues. The building pictured here was an addition to the plant finished in 1918. Diamond Match stayed in business until 1955. The land was sold to UW Oshkosh in the 1960s, and the buildings were all razed by the 1970s. (Author's collection.)

Founded in 1907, Waite Grass Carpet Company produced twine and grass carpets. A unique vegetation called wire grass, abundant in the Oshkosh area, was perfect for twine and carpet production. The company rebuilt its plant in 1910 on Custer Avenue and operated there until 1966. Added to the Wisconsin Register of Historic Places in 2018, this structure still stands. (Courtesy of Ron Metz.)

This postcard shows the Oshkosh Bottle Wrapper Company. It was on Ohio Street, near the south end of the Wisconsin Avenue Bridge. Oshkosh's former mayor William Dichmann founded the company in 1904. It produced bottle wrappers, hay mats, and excelsior packaging. The company remained in business until the 1970s. (Courtesy of Ron Metz.)

Oshkosh Brewing Company resulted from a merger of three local breweries in 1894. This postcard shows the brewery's plant that was built in 1911. Very much focused on local pride, the brewery heavily used Chief Oshkosh in its branding and marketing. The brewery's flagship product was Chief Oshkosh Beer, which was released as a "near beer" in 1928. The brewery survived Prohibition and remained open until 1971. (Courtesy of Ron Metz.)

Peoples Brewing Company was formed by South Side tavern owners who wanted to break Oshkosh Brewing Company's grip on the local market. It opened in 1913 on South Main Street. The company was bought by Theodore Mack in 1970, making it the first black-majority-owned brewery in America. The bottling department still stands. (Author's collection.)

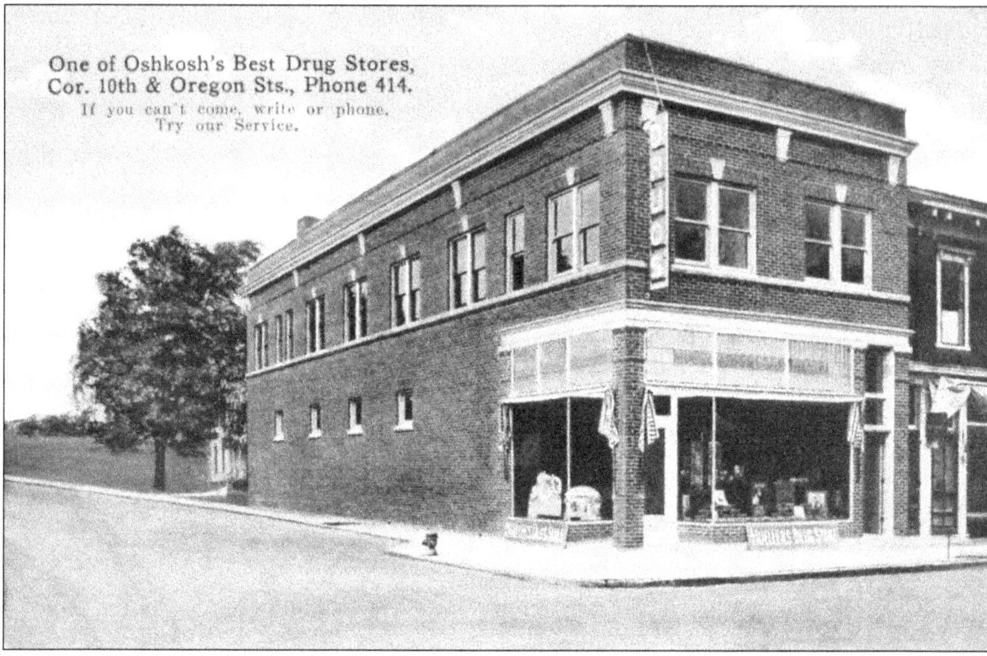

Frederick W. Mueller opened a drugstore in 1907. Following a fire in 1914, the drugstore had to be rebuilt. The rebuild is shown here. In 1918, Mueller partnered with Alfred Potter and formed Mueller Potter Drug Company. Their business grew and had up to five locations in Oshkosh over the years. No longer a drugstore, the building still stands. (Courtesy of WCHAS.)

Bauman's Drug Store, pictured on the left, was the first-floor tenant of the Beckwith House Hotel. At this time, it was common for Main Street buildings to be home to multiple businesses. The building was originally four stories. After a fire in 1880, Samuel Beckwith could only afford to restore the first two stories. Bauman's remained open until 1929. (Author's collection.)

Bemis-Hooper-Hays was a grocery store in downtown Oshkosh at 41 High Avenue. Founded by E.E. Bemis, Ben Hooper, and H.M. Hays, the store opened in 1901. Zinke Company bought out the store in 1934. The building was likely razed after its sale in 1945. There is no relation between E.E. Bemis and the Bemis Inc. that currently operates in Oshkosh. (Courtesy of Tristan Huss.)

Seymour Heyman emigrated from Germany as a young man. In 1884, he opened a dry goods store at 95 Main Street. His store was immensely successful. When Heyman retired in 1923, ownership was transferred to Henderson-Hoyt. Note that "The Greater Henderson-Hoyt Company" is in a different typeface. The postcard appears to have been restamped with the new name. This building became a Boston Store in 1945. (Author's collection.)

Stein's Shop, Oshkosh, Wis. The Most Unique in the World.

STEIN'S UNIQUE SHOP — OSHKOSH, WIS.

In 1911, Frank Stein opened a women's clothing store on Main Street. Operating downtown was expensive, so Stein decided to relocate. His decision to move into an elaborate mansion helped the store earn the nickname "The Most Unique Shop in the World." Stein selected a three-story mansion previously owned by George Gates, the manager of Diamond Match Company. The 1889 Victorian mansion offered an elegant setting for the business. In addition to selling women's fine clothing and gifts, the store also had four tea rooms. These amenities made shopping at Stein's an experience. Frank Stein ultimately pioneered the idea of having a retail store in a residential area. Stein's operated out of this mansion from 1924 until it burned down in 1947. (Both, author's collection.)

OshKosh B'Gosh successfully branded the city's name to represent its iconic overalls. OshKosh B'Gosh started as a workwear manufacturer in 1895. Its main clientele was farmers, along with railroad and industrial workers. Knowing the presence of a union-made label was important to their customers, early owners Howard Jenkins and James Clark invited the United Garment Workers of America onboard. Along with a union label, the OshKosh B'Gosh slogan was an important part of their product. The origins of the slogan are surrounded by lore, but the phrase was introduced to the company in 1911. The bib-style overalls were its most popular product. After the 1940s, the job market changed and fewer people needed heavy-duty workwear. The company shifted its focus to children's bib overalls, which became a success. This postcard shows a 16-foot-tall farmer wearing OshKosh B'Gosh overalls. One would assume this was in Oshkosh, Wisconsin. However, it was actually in Oshkosh, Nebraska, at a tourist booth. This community was founded by Oshkosh, Wisconsin, residents and was incorporated in 1910. (Author's collection.)

First National Bank is Oshkosh's oldest bank. Founded in 1852 by Darling, Wright, Kellogg & Company, it was originally located in J.W. Scott's jewelry store on the corner of Main and Otter Streets. The bank gained a state charter in 1857 and a national charter in 1863. In 1875, the bank moved to its current location on the corner of Main Street and Washington Avenue. Here, the bank was rebuilt three times. The first was a two-story Second Empire–style building. The postcard above shows the bank's second building, constructed in 1911. The postcard at left shows the bank that still stands today. It was built in 1927 and is one of the tallest buildings in Oshkosh. (Both, author's collection.)

The State Bank was near Ninth Avenue and Oregon Street. This card was likely used as a promotional tool for the bank. The back lists the bank's assets and liabilities and mentions that it pays three percent interest on time deposits. This building later became home to the Oshkosh Public Library's South Side Branch. The building still stands, and the facade now reads "Library" rather than "Bank." (Courtesy of WCHAS.)

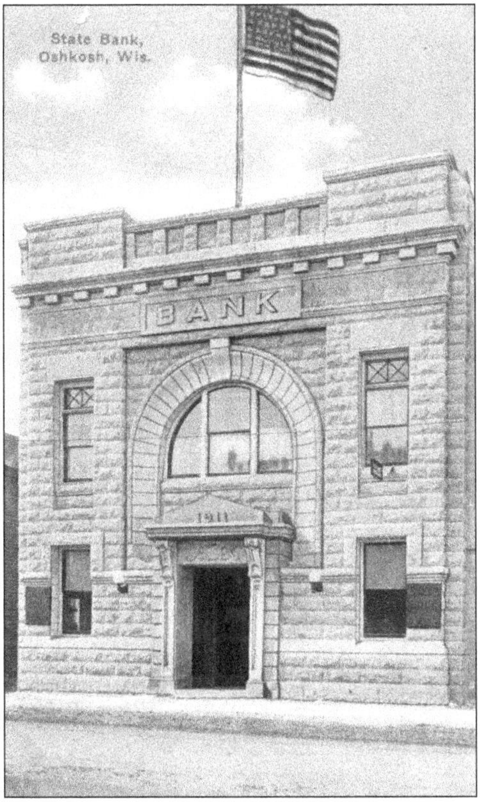

City National Bank dates to 1871. This postcard shows its second location, on the northeast corner of Main Street and Waugoo Avenue, which opened in 1922. City National Bank was forced to close during the Great Depression, but it reopened and reorganized as Old National Bank. This building was razed in 1977. (Courtesy of WCHAS.)

The Tremont House was one of Oshkosh's first hotels. Joseph Staudenraus opened the 25-room hotel in 1866 on the corner of State Street and Waugoo Avenue. In its early days, it charged between $1 and $1.25 per night. The Tremont was considered the area's finest hotel until the Athearn was built in 1891. This building remained a hotel until it was razed in 1962. (Author's collection.)

The original Revere Hotel burned down in 1877. This postcard showing the 1881 rebuild is labeled the New Revere Hotel. George Athearn was the hotel's manager in the late 1880s. The Revere remained open until 1919. The building was later converted for commercial use. It was razed in the early 1980s, creating space for the Oshkosh Convention Center, which was built in 1986. (Courtesy of Ron Metz.)

The Athearn Hotel was a significant part of downtown Oshkosh since 1891. When the building was razed in 1964, the rubble was used as fill to create Ki Ni Island. The island became the site of Oshkosh's new luxury hotel, the Pioneer Inn. Even though the Athearn Hotel no longer stands, the Soldiers Monument provides a reference to where it once stood. (Author's collection.)

The Pioneer Inn and Marina served as a luxury hotel for Oshkosh. It opened in 1965 and had three dining rooms, cocktail lounges, and 150 guest rooms. This hotel became one of Oshkosh's gems and stayed open until 2005. The complex was razed in sections, with the final one occurring in 2019. The future use of the site is uncertain. (Courtesy of Ron Metz.)

The Hotel Raulf was built in 1927. The 10-story hotel changed the skyline of Oshkosh's Main Street, along with its architectural style. The front facade featured Art Deco influences, giving this building a more exotic feel. Hotel Raulf was also home to the Strand Movie Theater and a basement bowling alley. It closed in 1981 and was converted into apartments. (Author's collection.)

Club Raulf opened as a nightclub attached to Hotel Raulf in 1936. The day before opening, the *Oshkosh Daily Northwestern* called Club Raulf "Wisconsin's Smartest and Finest Dine and Dance Club." (Author's collection.)

Four

Oshkosh on the Water

Nestled between Lake Butte des Morts and Lake Winnebago, with the Fox River running through it, Oshkosh is a city on the water. This waterfront location has always been advantageous for the people who lived here and is ultimately what allowed the area to be successful in the lumber industry. Aside from its location being useful, Oshkosh's waterways provided recreation and made for picturesque postcards. Vintage Oshkosh postcards capture the city's thriving boating scene. Steamships sailed the Fox River, and the city was also home to multiple boating and sailing clubs when this chapter's postcards were produced in the early 20th century. This chapter covers all things related to water, such as boats, beaches, bridges, steamships, and the inlets of Lake Winnebago, including Stoney Beach, Lake Rest, and Indian Point.

Oshkosh has a lengthy history with boating, both industrially and recreationally. Oshkosh's first business was actually water-related. James Knaggs operated a ferry between 1830 and 1850 that took passengers across the Fox River. Knagg's Ferry ran from modern-day Rainbow Park to Riverside Cemetery. Ferry service was important because it was the only way to cross the river before the Main Street Float Bridge was constructed in 1847. Steamships also played a role in transportation in Oshkosh. Since 1844, steamboats lined the Fox River shipping lumber, coal, and other goods. Steamships also had recreational value. Sunday cruises were an especially popular pastime in the early 1900s. The year 1923 marked the end of the steamboat era in Oshkosh, but not an end to water recreation. The city was home to multiple boating clubs, including the Oshkosh Yacht Club and the Oshkosh Powerboat Club. The yacht club was established in 1869 and held the first regatta on Lake Winnebago that same year. Oshkosh also has a surprisingly significant history in boat motor manufacturing, with two major manufactures, H.C. Doman and Universal Motor Company. Although this type of manufacturing has moved away from Oshkosh, the city is still a haven for recreational boaters.

Similar to Lake Winnebago, Lake Butte des Morts was originally marshland. When dams were installed downriver in Menasha in 1850, the Fox River rose and flooded these marshlands. The French name translates to "hill of the dead." The term's origins are surrounded by lore, tracing back to a supposed 1730s battle between the French and the Fox tribe. (Courtesy of WCHAS.)

The Oshkosh Power Boat Club was on Lake Butte des Morts and was organized in 1905. Members bonded over a love for boating but also worked to make more public landings and docks. The clubhouse was designed by Oshkosh architect George A. Rockwell. (Courtesy of WCHAS.)

Lake Butte des Morts was a recreational asset to the Oshkosh community. Oakwood, on the southeast side of the lake, was a common launching site for boaters. Oakwood was also a popular place to camp, relax, and enjoy the water. Here, a group of people can be seen fishing on the boat dock. (Courtesy of WCHAS.)

Parts of Lake Butte des Morts's shoreline came to be known as Waldwic because of the Sawyer family's summer home of that name. The original home was constructed in 1890 and was expanded in 1915. William Waters was the architect of the expansion project. The home still stands and is a private residence. (Courtesy of Ron Metz.)

Located on a river between two major lakes, Oshkosh was a bustling waterfront city with its share of riverboats and steamships. Scenes like this were common in the late 19th and early 20th centuries. This view shows the *Paul L.* approaching the Main Street Bridge. (Author's collection.)

Postcard views refer to this site as the city dock, boat docks, or Riverside Park. The area was previously the McKenzie and Crawford steamship dock and coal yard. The area became Riverside Park in 1910 but still operated as a public dock. (Author's collection.)

Passengers wait to board the *Thistle* at a boat landing in Oshkosh. Going for a Sunday cruise was a popular pastime. Excursion routes traced the Fox River and Lake Winnebago. For the *Thistle*, trips from Berlin and Calumet Harbor to Oshkosh were common. Berlin residents paid a 10¢ fare for the all-day, 32-mile trip. (Author's collection.)

The *Thistle* was constructed in 1864 and was originally named the *J.H. Crawford*. The boat was remodeled in 1899 and renamed. The 144-foot steamer was a cargo ship but was more popular as an excursion boat. (Author's collection.)

Colorized to give the appearance of night, this postcard shows the *Leander Choate II* docked at Riverside Park. Built in 1908, the steamer was the last of its kind constructed in the Oshkosh area. The 126-foot excursion boat was named after Oshkosh lumberman Leander Choate. Since it had a full second deck, it was considered the largest steamer built in the area. (Author's collection.)

In 1922, the *Leander Choate II* was expanded to 140 feet and renamed the *Valley Queen*. This remodel featured an enclosed dance floor on the second deck. Excursion cruising was an all-day event. Guests could enjoy food and entertainment along with the beautiful waterfront scenery. Unfortunately, the *Valley Queen* only sailed for one season before burning while in winter storage. (Author's collection.)

Constructed in 1907, the *Paul L.* was a 124-foot, three-deck steamer. Its typical excursion route ran from Oshkosh across Lake Butte des Morts, through Winneconne and Poygan, and up to the town of Tustin. The vessel had a 15-year run. After 1922, it was used primarily as a barge. It sank in 1924 in the Fox River by the Lawe Street Bridge in Appleton, and the wreckage is still present. (Courtesy of Ron Metz.)

The Oshkosh Avenue Bridge was once called the West Algoma Street Bridge, since this street was west of Algoma Boulevard. The street's name was changed to Oshkosh Avenue in the late 1950s. The bridge pictured here was constructed in 1913. This view shows the *Paul L.* passing through the bridge, and Paine Lumber Company buildings at right. (Author's collection.)

The Jackson-Oregon Street Bridge, pictured here, was constructed in 1919 to replace a swing bridge that was constructed in 1879. It was designed by the Chicago firm Scherzer Rolling Lift Bridge Company, which also designed the West Algoma Street Bridge. (Author's collection.)

This view highlights the bridge's elegance, including a public comfort station, an operator's house, and electric lighting. Morgan Company woodpiles can be seen to the left. Unfortunately, this bridge fell into disrepair by the mid-1950s. Rebuilt in 1956, it still stands today. (Courtesy of Ron Metz.)

The float bridge pictured here was built in 1849 and operated as a privately owned toll bridge. This was the first bridge to span the Fox River in Oshkosh. In 1854, it was bought by the city and became a free bridge. Even in the early 20th century there was an interest in historic postcard views, as evidenced by the popularity of this 1856 view. (Author's collection.)

During the construction of a new Main Street Bridge, the city ran a ferry service across the Fox River from 1904 to 1906. Prior to bridges, ferries were the main means of transportation between Oshkosh's north and south sides. Oshkosh pioneer Webster Stanley operated a ferry at this site starting in 1846. Ferry service was less needed once the first Main Street Bridge was built in 1849. (Author's collection.)

The Main Street Bridge was constructed in 1905. This was a swing bridge—the center part would rotate, rather than lift, to allow boats to come through. The bridge was designed by the Modern Steel Company of Waukesha. This bridge stood until 1971, when it was replaced with the current structure that stands today. (Courtesy of Ron Metz.)

This scene shows all the hustle and bustle surrounding the Main Street Bridge. Although it was the city's principal street, Main Street was first known as Ferry Street. Modern-day Algoma Boulevard was actually referred to as Main Street up until 1855, when the name was granted to the current Main Street downtown. (Author's collection.)

The Rockwell Light was designed by local architect George A. Rockwell for William Bray, a local resident who became a state senator in 1914. Bray was also an avid sailor. He acquired this lakefront property in 1907 and wanted a lighthouse to warn of the shallow reefs. Bray requested the government build a lighthouse at this location, but his request was denied. His wish came partially true in 1917 when his lighthouse became government licensed. The lighthouse was never officially named. The postcard above refers to it as the Rockwell Light, likely due to Rockwell's unexpected death in 1909 shortly before the lighthouse was completed. The postcard below refers to the scene as Bray's Point. The lighthouse has been decommissioned since the 1950s and is part of a private residence today. (Both, author's collection.)

The Oshkosh Yacht Club was established in 1869. Members originally met in a boathouse on the river. The club's permanent clubhouse was constructed on Lake Winnebago by Menominee Park in 1903. William Waters was the architect for the project. Postmarked 1907, this card shows a crowd watching the races. (Author's collection.)

During World War I, yacht club membership declined so much that the building was sold to the City of Oshkosh. The club was still able to use the building, but it was now known as the Municipal Club. The yacht club repurchased the building in 1927. Ownership switched again in 1929 with the onset of the Great Depression. (Author's collection.)

In 1932, Oshkosh's American Legion Cook Fuller Post No. 70 purchased the clubhouse. The building was now called the Legion on the Lake. Similar to before, the yacht club was able to use the building as its headquarters. In 2008, the Legion on the Lake underwent a massive renovation project. To honor its architect, William Waters, the owners renamed the building The Waters. (Courtesy of WCHAS.)

Even though the yacht club building was always switching hands, club members still had access to the docks. This scene shows docked sailboats, steam yachts, and a rowboat. (Courtesy of Ron Metz.)

This postcard shows a Doman motorboat on Lake Winnebago. The company originated as Union Iron Work Company in the 1880s. It reorganized as H.C. Doman Company in 1894 and produced a variety of motors and engines, becoming well known for its marine engines. Doman motors allowed boats a speed of anywhere from 5.5 to 20 miles per hour. (Courtesy of Ron Metz.)

The *North Butte* was a 38-foot speedboat owned by Richard Schell of Duluth, Minnesota. This boat won multiple races and was equipped with a Doman motor. As the card notes, it could travel up to 20 miles per hour, which was extremely fast in 1906. (Courtesy of WCHAS.)

Since 1900, the Wisconsin State Fish Hatchery had been located by the lagoon in Menominee Park. In 1916, the facility was moved to River Drive, now called Lake Shore Drive. The building was moved over frozen Lake Winnebago and massively remodeled. The goal was to make it a showplace facility for Oshkosh and the state of Wisconsin. (Courtesy of WCHAS.)

This postcard shows a dreamy view of Miller's Bay in Menominee Park. The bay was named after Col. Lucius Miller, who originally owned the land. Monkey Island is in the background. The yacht club constructed this island in 1913 to act as a breakwater. (Author's collection.)

This picturesque scene shows Indian Point on Lake Winnebago on Oshkosh's north side. In its early days, this land was mostly owned by Charles Nevitt, who worked for his father-in-law, George Paine, at the Paine Lumber Company as treasurer from 1893 to 1945. Today this is a lakefront residential area. (Courtesy of WCHAS.)

Located on Lake Winnebago, Oshkosh could boast charming scenes of sailboats on the open water. This postcard is colorized to depict a twilight view of the lake. (Courtesy of Ron Metz.)

South of Oshkosh along the shoreline of Lake Winnebago, Stoney Beach was a popular location for camping and swimming. Many postcards of this beach were produced. The current Stoney Beach Road refers to this location. (Courtesy of WCHAS.)

Lake Rest was not an actual lake but rather an inlet from Lake Winnebago. This scene shows a rowboat and a sailboat enjoying the calm waters. Today this area corresponds with Lake Rest Lane on the south side of Oshkosh. (Courtesy of WCHAS.)

The Pioneer Inn was located on Ki Ni Island, where the Fox River spills into Lake Winnebago. Built in 1965, this hotel offered prime access to Oshkosh's waterfront recreation. Guests could rent boats or paddleboats and enjoy cruising Lake Winnebago. Above is the hotel as boaters would see it. The postcard below gives a view of the hotel's fully equipped marina, which could hold up to 250 boats. It was the perfect location for docking and dining. The Pioneer even had a seaplane area, mixing Oshkosh's love for boating and aviation. (Both, courtesy of WCHAS.)

Five

Parks and Monuments

Parks and monuments enrich and beautify a city. Like in many communities, Oshkosh's parks are situated on the water, creating many opportunities for beautiful spaces and picturesque postcard images. The history of Oshkosh parks begins in the late 1880s, when North Park and South Park were established in conjunction. Col. Lucius Miller always considered his property along Lake Winnebago the prime location for a park. Miller offered to sell the land to the city, but no offers were accepted until Oshkosh mayor Ephraim Eldorus Stevens came along. Many citizens opposed the purchase, thinking the $25,000 price too high for the poor marshy land. To gain support for the purchase, Mayor Stevens also purchased Samuel Osborn's estate for a South Side park. Mayor Stevens was later voted out of office over these purchases. As the city grew, more parks were established including Riverside Park and Electric Park.

The installation of many of Oshkosh's statues and public monuments can be traced to one person, John Hicks. The John Hicks collection is unique because it is likely one of the largest given to a city by a single donor. Hicks (1847–1917) was the owner of the *Oshkosh Daily Northwestern* and Hicks Printing Company. During the planning process of the Oshkosh Public Library's new building, he helped fund the busts of library benefactors Marshall Harris and Philetus Sawyer. Hicks was also active in Republican politics. He was appointed minister to Peru in 1889 by Pres. Benjamin Harrison, and ambassador to Chile in 1905 by Pres. Theodore Roosevelt. Through his travels and work with the Oshkosh Public Library, Hicks gained a great interest in civic beautification, and sponsored public art to help promote Oshkosh as a cultured community. After his death in 1917, the John Hicks Trust Fund was established to fund future purchases as well as the maintenance of existing statues, busts, and monuments.

Menominee Park is Oshkosh's largest park, but it didn't always go by that name. Established in 1890, the park was previously known as North Park. The name change coincided with the placement and dedication of the Chief Oshkosh statue in 1911. In addition to commemorating Chief Oshkosh, the new name was meant to honor the Menominee Nation. This was the main tribe present in the early 1800s when American settlers arrived in the area. This name change occurred during the heyday of postcards. Many postcards of this park use the names interchangeably, as shown with these two cards. (Both, author's collection.)

Similar to today, the Merritt Street entrance was considered the main entrance to the park. This view shows the entrance marked with an arbor, which was constructed in 1905. (Author's collection.)

Menominee Park's beach was a popular swimming spot. It was also a place to relax and enjoy the lake. In this view, benches and canoes line the lakeshore. (Courtesy of WCHAS.)

The bathhouse at Menominee Park was a crucial part of the beachgoing experience. The park's first bathhouse was constructed in 1903. With the increasing number of beachgoers, that first facility was quickly outgrown. This postcard shows the new bathhouse that was completed in 1913. This facility contained 106 lockers, compared to 22 in the original bathhouse. (Courtesy of WCHAS.)

In 1928, the shoreline of Lake Winnebago at Menominee Park was greatly improved with the addition of a water toboggan slide. Initiated by the Oshkosh Junior Chamber of Commerce, this project was a big hit and a great thrill for beachgoers. (Author's collection.)

Menominee Park also had its own tourist camp. With the proliferation of automobiles in the 1920s and 1930s, Americans hit the road and traveled. Many communities had tourist camps that served as free rest spots. The Menominee Park tourist camp was closed in 1928 due to low usage. The camp reopened in 1936, but campers had to pay a fee. (Courtesy of WCHAS.)

In its early days, Menominee Park had a bandstand located where the Chief Oshkosh statue currently resides. When the statue was placed in 1911, the bandstand was moved to a more central point in the park. In the late 1920s, a larger replacement was needed. The bandstand shown here was designed by Henry Auler and was completed in the spring of 1928. (Author's collection.)

The Chief Oshkosh statue was created by Italian sculptor Chevalier Gaetano Trentanove. It was donated to the city in 1911 by John Hicks and was meant to honor the city's namesake. Although it was well-intended, the statue is not a true representation of Chief Oshkosh's physical appearance. Also, the accompanying placard does not fully acknowledge his achievements. (Author's collection.)

This Chief Oshkosh statue postcard shows the "gravesite" of Chief Oshkosh. In 1926, Oshkosh realtor Alfred McComb persuaded Chief Oshkosh's grandson Reginald Oshkosh to allow for the transfer of Oshkosh's body from the reservation to the park. On the reservation, the reburial was known as a hoax. The hoax did not become widely known by Oshkosh residents until a newspaper exposé in the 1970s. (Courtesy of WCHAS.)

Fr. Claude Allouez was a Jesuit missionary and one of the early French explorers of the Wisconsin region. This marker in Menominee Park commemorates the location where Allouez held the first Catholic Mass in Winnebago County in 1670. (Courtesy of WCHAS.)

This view shows the entrance to Menominee Park's lagoons from Millers Bay. Originally, a bridge connected these two parcels of land. The bridge was taken down in 1903 to allow for the first lagoon to be a sailboat harbor. A new bridge was constructed at the mouth of the second lagoon, also known as the narrows. (Courtesy of WCHAS.)

The lagoons at North Park proved to be a desirable place to go fishing and boating. In 1892, the swamps were filled in and the lagoons were dredged. This created peaceful spaces for recreation, as pictured in this postcard. A walking bridge across the narrows can be seen in the background. (Courtesy of WCHAS.)

The iron bridge shown in the previous card was replaced by this intricate limestone bridge in 1921, designed by Henry Auler. The bridge is named after World War I sergeant Cooper D. Wells. (Author's collection.)

The Menominee Park Zoo dates to 1945. Similar to today, the zoo's lagoon served as a duck pond. The zoo also had deer from the beginning. By 1947, it hosted more animals, including raccoons, skunks, and foxes. The zoo was redesigned in the late 1970s and dedicated as the Menominee Park Zoo in 1978. (Courtesy of WCHAS.)

Since its establishment, Menominee Park has always been a place for Oshkosh residents to relax and enjoy Lake Winnebago. This view from the 1960s shows a boat-lined lakeshore. (Courtesy of WCHAS.)

The Carl Schurz monument, located in Menominee Park, was donated to the city of Oshkosh by John Hicks in 1914. Schurz was the first German-born American to become a US senator, representing Missouri from 1869 to 1875. Many considered Schurz a great German American and an "Apostle of Democracy." Many Wisconsinites were awed and inspired by Schurz, including John Hicks. (Author's collection.)

The George Washington monument is a replica of Jean Antoine Houdon's marble Washington statue that resides at Virginia's capitol. Two replicas were made. One was acquired by Hicks, and the other went to Versailles in France. Hicks donated this statue in 1911. It was originally located by the park's lagoons. In 1957, the statue was moved to its current location on Hazel Street and Menominee Drive. (Author's collection)

The Soldier's Monument commemorates the Wisconsin men who fought for the Union in the Civil War. This monument was dedicated in 1907 and was the first of many to be presented to the city of Oshkosh by Col. John Hicks. The statue was created by Italian sculptor Gaetano Trentanove and is considered his crowning work. The statue cost Hicks $10,000. In the past, the street layout by the Grand Opera House was different. The monument was originally on a grass plot known as Monument Square. This square was essentially the intersection of High, Market, and Division Streets. The image below provides perspective on the statue's previous surroundings. The buildings in the background no longer stand. The Soldiers Monument is now on the corner of the expanded Opera House Square. (Both, author's collection.)

The Hiker monument was made possible by John Hicks's trust fund and Nathan Paine's land donation. Dedicated in 1939, this monument was created in honor of the veterans of the Spanish-American War. It has always been located on Algoma Boulevard across from the Paine Art Center & Gardens. The back of the postcard reads, "The Hiker, emblematic of American Ideals represents the service men of 1898." (Courtesy of WCHAS.)

John Hicks donated the Lincoln Monument to the city of Oshkosh in 1909. The bust is based on the upper portion of a full-size statue by Adolph Alexander Weinman. That statue resides at Lincoln's birthplace in Kentucky. The bust was unveiled in front of Lincoln Elementary School in 1909. It was relocated to the Oshkosh Public Museum in 2017. (Courtesy of Tristan Huss.)

Riverside Park is on the Fox River adjacent to the Main Street Bridge. The land was donated to the city of Oshkosh by Wisconsin state senator William Bray in 1909. Riverside Park was a favorite lounge spot for Oshkosh residents. (Author's collection.)

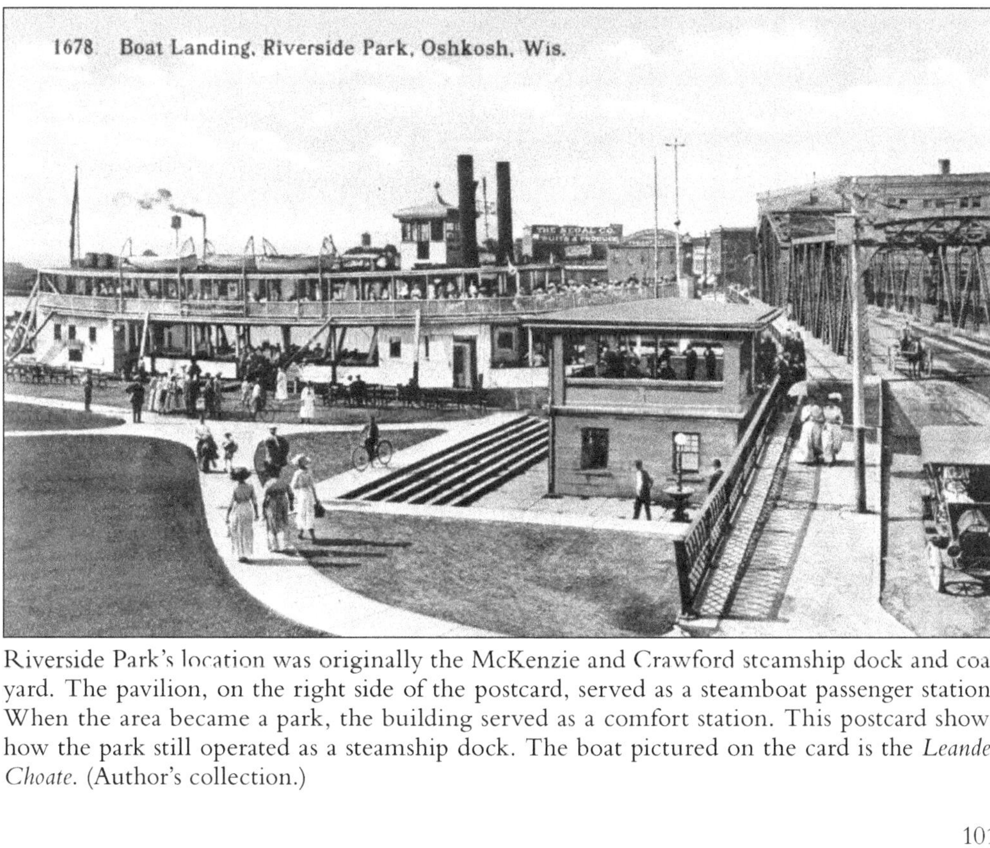

Riverside Park's location was originally the McKenzie and Crawford steamship dock and coal yard. The pavilion, on the right side of the postcard, served as a steamboat passenger station. When the area became a park, the building served as a comfort station. This postcard shows how the park still operated as a steamship dock. The boat pictured on the card is the *Leander Choate*. (Author's collection.)

The City of Oshkosh purchased the land for South Park from Samuel Osbourn in 1889. This purchase was meant to complement the North Park purchase. Mayor E.E. Stevens's purchase was unfavorable with Oshkosh residents, and he was voted out at the end of his term. However, in the long run, gaining two parks was a win for the city of Oshkosh. (Courtesy of WCHAS.)

South Park was originally known as Osbourn Woods. Throughout the 1890s, this 16-acre parcel was improved for recreation with the dredging of artificial lagoons. The iron bridge in the background was added in 1910. Surrounded by residential areas from its beginnings, South Park proved to be a popular gathering place for Oshkosh south-siders. (Author's collection.)

This view of South Park shows the park's first stone bridge, which was built in 1912. The bridge was reconstructed in 1920 and still stands today. (Author's collection.)

This view shows some of the park's amenities. A circular swing can be seen on the left. The cannon at center was obtained in 1899 from the Rock Island Arsenal. In 1936, it was moved to the Oshkosh Public Museum, and it has since been on display outside the main entrance. The building on the right is the park house, which was originally Samuel Osbourn's home. (Author's collection.)

This view shows the electric streetcar rails that led to the entrance of White City Park. The park was started in 1898 by the Citizens Traction Company about three miles south of the city. Streetcar companies typically built parks at city limits to promote usage of streetcars on the weekends. The fare from any point in Oshkosh to White City was 5¢. (Courtesy of WCHAS.)

Electric Park had many amenities, including a band stand, a sand beach, a bathhouse, an outdoor theater, and a dance pavilion, which is pictured on this postcard. The park operated from 1898 to 1954 under three different names. Over its lifespan, it was known as Electric Park, White City Park, Electric Park again, and finally EWECO Park. (Courtesy of WCHAS.)

Electric Park's major draw was that it was, in fact, electric. For many Oshkosh residents, visiting Electric Park at night was an especially mesmerizing experience. (Courtesy of WCHAS.)

The Shoot-the-Chutes water slide can be seen in the background of this postcard behind the rustic bridge. This waterslide was 40 feet high. Riders took toboggans down the 125-foot-long slide and were shot into the water. This was an especially popular ride during hot summer months. (Courtesy of WCHAS.)

This postcard shows a two-story, open-air dance pavilion designed by William Waters. It was one of the park's major attractions, lasting until the 1950s. When the park first opened, Waters also designed a summer theater, two bandstands, and two refreshment booths. (Author's collection.)

The roller coaster at White City was among the park's most popular attractions. Constructed in 1906, the coaster was built in a figure-eight. For 5¢, visitors could ride through nearly a mile's worth of track in a mere 45 seconds. (Courtesy of WCHAS.)

Midways are the areas of fairs or circuses with carnival games and sideshows. A banner in the background of this postcard promotes a minstrel show. Popular in the early 20th century, these shows featured a variety of skits typically performed by white actors in blackface. Today, they are considered racist and demeaning. (Courtesy of WCHAS.)

New White City Park was opened by the Bijou Amusement Company in 1906. Similar in name, this park was located on 10 acres near the existing White City Park. New White City's most popular attraction was its baseball diamond. After one year of separate operation, the two parks merged and became White City. (Author's collection.)

The city's first cemetery was Locust Grove, on the corner of Wisconsin Street and Algoma Boulevard. Locust Grove was quickly outgrown. Land was purchased for a new cemetery, named Riverside, in 1855. This view shows Riverside's main entrance. The sexton's cabin can be seen to the right. This cabin was moved across Algoma Boulevard in 1920 to make room for the cemetery chapel. (Author's collection.)

The Riverside Cemetery fountain featured Hebe, daughter of Zeus and goddess of eternal youth. The fountain was erected in 1892 to beautify the cemetery. It was later razed to make room for the chapel, which was completed in 1921. (Courtesy of WCHAS.)

This postcard shows a family gathered by a large tent at Stoney Beach. South of Oshkosh along the shoreline of Lake Winnebago, Stoney Beach was a popular location for camping and swimming. (Courtesy of WCHAS.)

Also known as Garlic Island, Island Park has a colorful history. During the War of 1812, the island was a British encampment. In the late 1880s, it was essentially a summer resort. Elite Oshkosh citizens built their own cabins here. During the production of this postcard in the early 1900s, Oshkosh businessman Stephen Radford bought up the majority of the island and vacationed here with his family. (Courtesy of Ron Metz.)

The Northern State Hospital Zoo dates to 1900. The zoo began when Dr. William A. Gordon, the hospital's superintendent, was gifted a badger by S.M. Eaton of Watertown and four English pheasants by Clyde Buckstaff of Oshkosh. Between 1902 and 1910, the zoo grew to include other animals. It was located in the back of the hospital and brought much joy and entertainment to the patients. Over time, Dr. Gordon's wild animal menagerie included a fox, a raccoon, two coyotes, seven elk, one wild pig, two Muscovy ducks and three dozen other ducks, a bulldog, pigeons, and an eagle. Dr. Gordon was a major supporter of the zoo, believing it made hospital life more fulfilling for the patients. It remained until about 1938. (Both, courtesy of Ron Metz.)

Six

Community Treasures

Oshkosh is a community with a variety of treasures ranging from institutions of higher learning to historic and cultural centers. Postcards are especially good for highlighting these treasures. There are places unique to Oshkosh, making it an enriching place to live. These include UW Oshkosh, the Grand Opera House, the public library, the public museum, the Paine Art Center & Gardens, Experimental Aircraft Association (EAA), and the Winnebago County Historical and Archeological Society.

The postcards in this chapter show UW Oshkosh's progression from a normal school to the university it is today. Oshkosh's large population relative to the rest of the state helped it become home to the state's third normal school in 1871. As Wisconsin's second largest city, Oshkosh wanted to establish itself as a cultural stronghold. The Grand Opera House was created to provide a grand entertainment venue. The Oshkosh Public Library was created to serve as a community gathering place dedicated to sharing knowledge and resources. The public library once hosted a museum room. The Winnebago County Historical Society, founded in 1919, helped expand the museum room's collections. It also strove to preserve the county's history, much like it does today. The museum room found a new home when Edgar Sawyer donated his residence to the city. Since opening in 1924, the Oshkosh Public Museum has continued to enrich the community by preserving and telling the story of Oshkosh's history.

As time passed, Oshkosh gained more institutions and traditions. The Paine Art Center & Gardens opened to the public in 1947. This treasure continues to enrich and inspire the community with its art, gardens, and architecture. Oshkosh also became a community with a focus on innovation. The annual EAA convention found its home in Oshkosh in 1969. Each year, thousands of aviation enthusiasts come to Oshkosh to celebrate the spirit of aviation. As in the past, these community treasures are still depicted on postcards today.

William Waters was commissioned to design Oshkosh's normal school, which was constructed from Calumet brick in the Second Empire style and featured a 144-foot tower. Construction began in 1868 and was completed in 1870. A lack of funds prevented the school from opening until 1871. It had multiple recitation rooms, a gymnasium, a model school, and a library. Surrounding landscaping, such as the water fountain below, also contributed to the building's charm. The original building was expanded multiple times. It stood until 1916, when it was destroyed by fire. Students and faculty saved as many books and artifacts as possible. Interestingly, students only missed one day of school. Classes were held in area churches and at Oshkosh's high school until Dempsey Hall was completed in 1917. (Both, author's collection.)

This postcard is labeled "State Teachers College." The building was intended to be an extension of the original normal school but served as its replacement instead. The school gained authority to award baccalaureate degrees in 1927, making it a college. In 1952, the building was renamed after Edward Dempsey, a member of the normal school board of regents. (Author's collection.)

Harrington Hall was originally an industrial arts building. The normal school expanded its teacher training programs and built this specialized facility in 1912. Courses were popular and attracted many male students to campus. Harrington Hall later served as the science building until Halsey Science Center was built in 1963. (Author's collection.)

The first student union for Oshkosh State Teachers College was a donation from Mary Reeve Franker. She donated her Algoma Boulevard home to serve as a social center and requested it be named after her grandfather Thomas Reeve. Opened in 1951, this facility was quickly outgrown. Reeve Union, as it is known today, opened in 1959 at a different location. (Author's collection.)

Starting in the 1950s, the Oshkosh State Teachers College expanded its programs. Offering more liberal arts degrees, the institution was renamed Wisconsin State College Oshkosh. More expansion and name changes followed. In 1963, when a graduate program was added, the college became a state university. In 1971, it became UW Oshkosh. (Author's collection.)

Grand Opera House—Oshkosh, Wis.

The Grand Opera House's lavish interior and exterior helped build up Oshkosh's reputation as a cultural stronghold in Wisconsin. The Grand opened in 1883 with *The Bohemian Girl* as the first production. Fond Du Lac native Abbie Carrington played the lead part. The Grand hosted notable acts over the years, including the Marx Brothers, John Phillip Sousa and his band, Harry Houdini, and Samuel Clemens (Mark Twain). The Grand Opera House also featured vaudeville acts and motion pictures. Years later, the building operated as an X-rated movie theater. Citizens wanted to see it put to better use, and a referendum was proposed to determine if the city should save the Grand. After the referendum passed, the City of Oshkosh acquired and restored the building to its original grandeur in the 1980s. Today, the Grand is the oldest operating opera house in the state of Wisconsin, and it continues to enhance the Oshkosh community by serving as a center for the performing arts. (Author's collection.)

The public library, pictured in these postcards, would not have been possible without Marshall and Abbie Harris. After Marshall's death in 1890, Abbie finalized plans for their $75,000 estate to be donated to the city for a public library on the condition that the city match their donation within three years. The city accepted and raised money through bonds and private donors, including Sen. Philetus Sawyer. The library opened in 1900. Board member John Hicks wanted to commemorate the generosity of these two major donors, so he commissioned Preston Powers to create marble busts of Marshall Harris and Philetus Sawyer. One bust can be seen in the background below. In 1911, eleven years after the building's completion, Hicks commissioned Gaetano Trentanove to create two bronze lions for the front entrance. (Both, author's collection.)

Showcasing and preserving local history binds a community together. Starting in 1905, a museum room was housed in the Oshkosh Public Library. As collections grew, this space became outgrown. Edgar P. Sawyer donated his home to the city in 1922 with the stipulation that it be used for the benefit of the public. The city had multiple ideas about what the home should be used for, including a children's hospital, a civic center, a junior high school, and a specialty school. Although unpopular, another idea was to raze the building and construct an auditorium. The city decided that a public museum would be the best use of the estate. In 1924, the building opened as the Art Museum, Sawyer Foundation. By 1929, the institution started going by its current name. The Oshkosh Public Museum is one of the state's oldest public museums, second only to the Milwaukee Public Museum. (Author's collection.)

These two views from the 1930s provide an idea of what the Oshkosh Public Museum looked like in its early days. When the museum opened, the first floor was reserved for art and the second floor for local history. The mural *Genus of Oshkosh* by Eugene Savage can be seen above on the right. This painting explains the city's origins and development. It centers on a Native American man surrounded by figures representing the city's agricultural, commercial, industrial, and intellectual development. Exhibits changed with time, showcasing the community's past for a present-day audience. The Pioneer Room, shown below, was an exhibit that explained Oshkosh's early history. (Both, courtesy of WCHAS.)

The Oshkosh Public Museum used to host a variety of extra historic buildings outside the Sawyer home. A fire barn is shown on the left, and a railroad depot is on the right. The landscape of the museum looks different today, since these buildings no longer stand. The fire barn was dismantled in 2018, as it had become unsafe for artifact storage. (Courtesy of WCHAS.)

The Apostle Clock is one of the most iconic objects in the Oshkosh Public Museum's collection. It was built in 1895 by local craftsman Mathias Kitz. This clock puts on an hourly show with music and lights. The 12 apostles rotate around the clock and bow to Jesus, all except Judas. This clock is a fine example of Wisconsin folk art. (Courtesy of WCHAS.)

The Paine Art Center & Gardens was originally intended to be the home of Nathan and Jessie Paine. Nathan was the third-generation owner of the Paine Lumber Company, and Jessie was the daughter of Kimberly-Clark founder John A. Kimberly. The couple wanted to build a showplace home that could also serve as a cultural center for the public. Construction on this English-style country estate began in 1927. The Great Depression slowed progress, stretching the project out nearly 20 years. Nathan Paine passed away in 1947, and Jessie chose not to live in the mansion alone. She oversaw the formation of the private, nonprofit organization that would sustain the art center. The Paine Art Center officially opened to the public in 1948. Jessie Paine served as president until her death in 1973 at the age of 100. (Both, courtesy of WCHAS.)

The Paines always intended for their home to have an art gallery that could be open to the public. The couple primarily collected French Barbizon and American landscape paintings. The Paines also had a considerable collection of work by Oshkosh artist Helen Farnsworth Mears. This postcard shows pieces from the Paines' personal collection, including Mears's sculpture *The Urn*, which is displayed in the center of the gallery. (Courtesy of WCHAS.)

The Paine mansion is an art piece in itself. The staircase was created by the studio of Alois Lang, a Bavarian master carver in Michigan. Nathan Paine had oak panels from the Paine Lumber Company sent to Lang's studio. The panels are entirely hand carved and took 10 months to create. Since there are three distinct styles of acorns and oak leaves, there were likely three carvers on the project. (Courtesy of WCHAS.)

The Paine mansion was built with the intention of serving as a fine example of architecture and art. The dining room is one of many elaborate rooms in the house. Notable is the George Washington portrait at left, attributed to Gilbert Stuart, a famous early American portraitist. (Courtesy of WCHAS.)

Along with being an art gallery and a historic home, the Paine Art Center & Gardens is also home to an elaborate botanical garden. This geometric formal garden was constructed in 1973 and is essentially a replica of the Dutch Pond Garden at Hampton Court in England. The pictured formal garden was removed in 2012 to make room for a new conservatory building. In 2017, a new formal garden was constructed with the remaining space. (Courtesy of WCHAS.)

The Experimental Aircraft Association was established in 1953 by Paul Poberezny. This organization for aviation enthusiasts promoted the use of homebuilt aircraft. The EAA held an annual convention that started in Milwaukee and then moved to Rockford, Illinois. The annual event outgrew both locations. In 1969, EAA found its new home in Oshkosh through the suggestion of local aviator and EAA member Steve Wittman. Today, EAA AirVenture is the world's largest aviation event. (Courtesy of WCHAS.)

With its large surrounding acreage that could accommodate thousands of campers, Oshkosh was the perfect place to hold the convention. During EAA week, Camp Scholler becomes a city within a city, boasting 11,600 campsites. This postcard scene from the 1970s shows the tent city and gives an idea of the immense number of campers. (Courtesy of WCHAS.)

Oshkosh was well suited for the convention, because it had two lengthy runways that did not cross, allowing many planes to land at once. During EAA week, Oshkosh has the busiest airport in the world. Today, the convention boasts 10,000 airplanes and over 600,000 visitors. (Courtesy of WCHAS.)

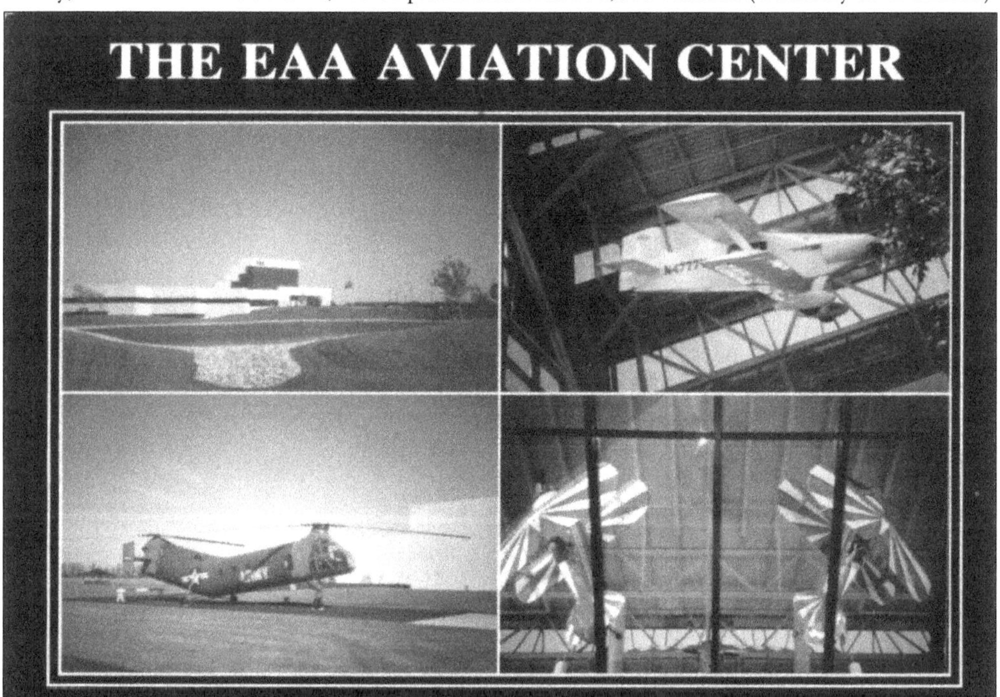

The EAA Aviation Center opened in 1983. It hosts EAA's headquarters and museum. (The previous museum was closer to the original convention grounds in Milwaukee.) The museum was a $10 million project and is one of the world's finest aviation attractions. (Courtesy of WCHAS.)

This postcard is of the Morgan House, which has been the headquarters of the Winnebago County Historical and Archeological Society since 1987. Originally, this 1884 Queen Anne–style home was John R. Morgan's residence. Morgan was one of the founders of the Morgan Company. The home cost $12,000 to construct and was considered one of the finest in Oshkosh. The Morgan family owned it until the 1940s. Next, it was owned by Constance Misky, who operated a cosmetology school on the first floor. In 1983, the home was listed in the National Register of Historic Places. In 1987, it became home to WCHAS. The society was founded in 1919 to research, preserve, and communicate the history of Winnebago County. Since its inception, WCHAS has been responsible for designating and preserving historical and archeological sites across the county. It continues to fulfill this mission today, sharing the county's history with community members. (Courtesy of WCHAS.)

Harold Helm (1927–1994) was a third-generation Oshkosh resident. Helm served with the US Navy from 1945 to 1946 and then finished his education at Oshkosh High School, graduating in 1947. He married Neva Bork in 1954 and the couple had four children. Harold Helm worked for Coca Cola Bottling Company and then UW Oshkosh in the Buildings and Grounds Department. He had many history-related hobbies, including genealogy and coin collecting. He owned Oshkosh-specific coin and banknotes but would collect just about anything Oshkosh-related. In the 1980s, he joined the Winnebago County Historical and Archeological Society and the Souvenir Card Collectors Society. By the time he passed away, his collection contained about 600 cards. (Both, author's collection.)

Bibliography

Cross, Scott. *Like a Deer Chased by Dogs: The Life of Chief Oshkosh*. Oshkosh, WI: Oshkosh Public Museum, 2002.

Domer, Randy. *We Shall Never Pass This Way Again*. Indianapolis, IN: Dog Ear Publishing, 2018.

———. *Yesterday in Oshkosh, My Hometown*. Indianapolis, IN: Dog Ear Publishing, 2012.

Goc, Michael. *Oshkosh at 150*. Friendship, WI: New Past Press Inc., 2003.

Groth, David, and Patti Pata. *A Compilation of Articles Pertaining to the Work of Architect William Waters*. Oshkosh, WI: Winnebago County Historical and Archaeological Society, 2000.

historicoshkosh.org

La Point, Ron. *Oshkosh: Preserving the Past*. Indianapolis, IN: Dog Ear Publishing, 2012.

Mercy School of Nursing Commemorative Yearbook, 1908–1982. Oshkosh, WI: Mercy Medical School of Nursing, 1982.

Mitchell, Don. *Steamboats on the Fox River*. Oshkosh, WI: Castle-Pierce Press, 1986.

Mueller, Joan. *Architecture and Art of the Oshkosh Public Library: A History and Guide*. Oshkosh, WI: Oshkosh Public Library, 2000.

Naleid, James. *Celebrating a Century as the Genuine Article: The Story of OshKosh B'Gosh, 1895–1995*. Lyme, CT: Greenwich Publishing Group Inc., 1995.

Oshkosh Centennial Inc. *Oshkosh: One Hundred Years a City, 1853–1953*. Oshkosh, WI: Castle Pierce Printing Company, 1953.

Oshkosh of Today. Oshkosh, WI: *Oshkosh Daily Northwestern*, 1898.

Public Monuments, Parks, and Art: Gifts Given the City of Oshkosh. Oshkosh, WI: *Oshkosh Daily Northwestern*, 1919.

Reiherzer, Lee. *Winnebago County Beer*. Charleston, SC: The History Press, 2019.

Tiedje, Edward. *History of Oshkosh Schools Past and Present*. Oshkosh, WI: Park N' Print Inc., 2004.

www.ingramcontent.com/pod-product-compliance
Lightning Source LLC
LaVergne TN
LVHW071101050926
847404LV00038B/478

* 9 7 8 1 4 6 7 1 0 5 2 2 4 *